FIVEFATHERS

*Five Australian Poets of
the Pre-Academic Era*

*presented and edited by
Les Murray*

Fyfield Books

First published in 1994 by
Carcanet Press Limited
208-212 Corn Exchange Buildings
Manchester M4 3BQ

A CIP catalogue record for this book
is available from the British Library.
ISBN 1 85754 087 5

The publisher acknowledges financial assistance
from the Arts Council of Great Britain

Set in 10pt Palatino by Bryan Williamson, Frome
Printed and bound in England by SRP Ltd, Exeter

FIVEFATHERS

Contents

5

JAMES McAULEY

FRANCIS WEBB

Introduction

This book presents to British and European readers selections from the work of five leading Australian poets of the generation before mine. All are men, and a parallel book for leading Australian women poets of the same period, edited by a woman, is envisaged for the future. Their case is arguably a little less urgent, as two of the very best, Judith Wright and Gwen Harwood, are happily still alive and have volumes of their collected poems currently in print in the United Kingdom. The men in this collection are all revered figures among poetry readers in Australia, part of a Golden Age in Australian poetry which paradoxically coincided with its greatest marginalisation. Each of the five, however, has hitherto been denied the international recognition I would have thought his obvious due. None of the five has had a complete collection of his work published in Britain. If these epitomes of their work alert British or European readers to the several excellences of these poets, perhaps a juster distribution of their work among its natural English-speaking public may belatedly come about.

In a spirit of free trade shaped as much as anything by the worldwide spread of the English language, I take it as natural that all poetry in our common language should be available wherever the language is spoken. The forces of cultural nationalism ranged against this idea are at bottom protectionist and unsure, however exalted they may be made to sound. For most of my life, and for all the lifetimes of the poets I am presenting here, older Empire conceptions of who should produce the Culture and who should reverently receive it were pretty immovably embodied in education and publishing alike. It is possible to see all criticism published before the 1980's as invalid, because based on an incomplete survey of its subject matter. Over the last decade or two, there has been a revolt against this. It is probably the greatest legacy of the university age that, having long maintained the hegemony of Western and motherland literature, it was able to revolutionize its own criticism and admit ex-colonial literatures by way of the new discipline usually called Commonwealth Lit or some similar name. In hindsight, such a development was

11

always inherent in the admission of vernacular literature of any sort to the purview of academic study, but it still had to be realized. The need for ever new subject matter, plus ideological disarmament against the claims of Black literature, both naturally helped the cause of non-Black writers too, but that does not lessen our debt of gratitude.

So far, the revolt against Empire conceptions has been more effective and thoroughgoing in education than in publishing. Australia is still a marketing 'territory' to the book trade. No publisher domiciled in Australia has been able to penetrate the British market. Export costs are prohibitive, and the Empire mindset would still bar any book lacking metropolitan approval from getting any bookshop orders. Multinational houses do now pick up the odd author not resident in Europe, and a few Australian writers and poets, almost vanishingly few, are published by houses which essentially operate solely in Britain and Europe. The same is true of the other empire centred in New York, and of course the Pope's Line that demarcates the British Traditional Market Zone from the American remains firmly on the map. If there are some glimmerings of hope for a few live authors, however, it is still barely on the horizon of the thinkable to do justice retroactively, and give what should always have been natural distribution to past authors from the former colonies. These are taken, almost without thinking about it, to have missed their moment through their own fault, and are crowded out by the ever-renewing vogues of New and Now.

Doing justice to every occurrence of poetic value, which is the great critical task I can't see any way of modifying or reducing, is going to require a good deal of help from publishers, now that the university age seems to be ending. By that term I mean that brief era of strong academic involvement in literature which grew into a rivalry with it and now seems to be deconstructing itself. In the future, I think, the supports of poetry will tend to be commercial publishing and the ever-growing phenomenon of public readings, which perhaps ten times more people will attend than will buy a book of verse. There have also been some tentative but successful forays into television, and radio has long been a

12

friend to our enterprise – or at least State and local radio have been; commercial radio, at least in Australia, will not have a bar of us. Denials of the existence of such a thing as literary value on the part of academics can probably be taken as a relinquishment by them of the job of evaluation, and the vacancy will probably be filled in the short term by newspaper and magazine critics, in the longer term by poets and readers. Increasingly, the networks of poetry are likely to grow away from the publish-or-perish specialist journals that were always more important in Australia and North America than in Britain anyway.

All five poets represented in this book are now dead. All of them began writing and publishing long before the university age – or before the benefits of that age were extended to Australian authors, even in their own country. Before the early 1960s, there was literature aplenty on university courses in our country, but it was not Australian literature. Australian poetry was tended and run by the poets themselves, through the weekly *Bulletin* newspaper, through other magazines which came and went, through reviews (but rarely publication of poems) in the ordinary metropolitan weekly newspapers, through one or two toeholds in the-then Australian Broadcasting Commission and, most importantly, through publication of books by Angus and Robertson and a handful of other houses. It was a thin, marginal time for poetry. An older nexus with the wider public had been broken, book sales were abysmal, and the newspapers which had once carried verse as a matter of course had long since dropped it. And yet this unpromising time, say from the 1930s to the beginning of the academic and radical age in the 1960s, produced a flowering of poetry in this country which no other period has excelled nor, I think, matched. One difference between that bare yet bountiful age and the next is that it tended to regard poetry as a given, a source of value in itself, while the next age was Hegelian, stressing notions of progress in society and art, or demanding the drama of revolutionary breakthroughs. Another difference may be that in the mid-century an earlier turmoil of peoples and influences in Australia achieved a moment of coherence and rest, before entering upon another period of complex change that still continues. All five men survived into the university age, and all but Kenneth Slessor published substantially in the politico-literary quarterlies which admitted Australian poetry before the universities did. Slessor edited one of these, and kept it apolitical, which annoyed some of its sponsors. Alone of the five, James McAuley became a literary academic and took part in the beginnings of Australian literature studies; he would go on to produce a good critical survey titled *A Map of Australian Verse*. David Campbell became part of the literary life around the Australian National University in Canberra, but as a poet, never as a teacher. The working lives of all five were spent before the days of the Literature Board and greatly increased government patronage of the arts; only Roland Robinson benefited from that, surviving long enough to hold an Emeritus Fellowship from the Literature Board in his declining years.

As in other anthologies I have edited, I have made poetic value paramount over such secondary concerns as biography, literary history, critical evaluation and the ranking imperative which assigns six poems to X because Y has eight and on that scale Z is worth only one. This is the mental world of the survey anthology, which has not served Australian literature particularly well overseas, and all such concerns lead back into variants of that imperial trap of exclusion against which this book is in revolt. My criticism, such as it is, of the work of these five distinguished colleagues of mine is all implicit in my personal selections of their verse. There, I have sought to show them off at their best and in generous measure, while leaving plenty over for interested readers to follow up – and so as not to pre-empt the complete book for the metropolitan market which each man's work still deserves. I have not presumed to proportion the amounts of space I have given the poets, and I make no statement of preference between them. Each has his own devoted partisans in Australia, plus a few abroad who have loved poetry enough to survey its whole range and discover them. Because they are not yet familiar abroad, I have provided brief biographical sleeve notes, though without, I hope, saying anything intrusive or directive about their writing. In one case, where a particular side of a man's work appealed to

14

me less than its other sides, I have declared the fact. Finally, I have not provided a glossary. I take it that all variants of English capable of equal subtlety and expressiveness are in fact equal, and that working out each other's lexis and usage is part of the fun of having a polycentric language.

Thanks are due, and gladly given, to my agent Margaret Connolly for her work in obtaining rights to the work of these five poets, and to Gwenda Jarred, the Rights and Permissions manager of Harper-Collins, holders of all Angus and Robertson rights from the past. For the poems of Roland Robinson, acknowledgement is made of the publishers A.W. and A.H. Reed, as well as Kardoorair Press, Island Press and Edwards & Shaw Ltd. I am also grateful to Jamie Grant for obtaining various hard-to-find books and checking a number of facts, and to my wife Valerie for reams of photocopying, for reading my typescript for errors, and for all her usual wise support and kindness. My thanks go to the heirs and assigns of the five for their generous permission to reprint these poems. Who knows? They may yet help to make Overseas a bigger country.

Kenneth Slessor

Of German Jewish and Hebridean Scottish ancestry, Kenneth Adolphe Schloesser was born at Orange, in central western New South Wales, on 27 March 1901. His father changed the family name to Slessor in 1914, but there is some evidence that the boy suffered discrimination for his German antecedents during the First World War. In 1920, he joined the Sydney *Sun* as a reporter, and he remained a journalist all his working life. Joining the staff of the popular offbeat Sydney paper *Smith's Weekly* in 1927, he rose to be its editor-in-chief in the late 1930s. From 1940 to 1944 he served as a War Correspondent with the Australian forces in Greece, Syria, Libya, Egypt and New Guinea; he 'retired hurt', in his own words, from this assignment after clashes with General Sir Thomas Blamey, the Australian Army commander. After the war, as well as being leader writer and literary editor of the Sydney Telegraph newspapers, he edited the literary journal *Southerly* and served for many years on the board of the Commonwealth Literary Fund, dispensing to writers such government patronage as then existed and more than once defending those denied funding for Cold War political reasons. Kenneth Slessor was married twice and had one son, and he died just after his seventieth birthday in 1971.

Many consider Slessor the greatest of all Australian poets, and are puzzled by the failure of his work so far to achieve recognition in the wider world. Adamantly opposed in his maturity to the older Australian ballad tradition, he began as an enthusiastic member of the anti-modernist circle which produced *Vision* magazine in Sydney in the early 1920s; this Bohemian grouping was under the vigorous influence of the vitalist painter and arts guru Norman Lindsay, whom Barry Humphries has called, in tribute to a famous Sydney confectionery firm, the 'Darrell Lea of eroticism'. Slessor outgrew this influence without rancour or any breach of his friendship with Lindsay. Though he became profoundly well read in contemporary European and American poetry, he always retained the antiquarian passion which the two men had shared. Between 1924 and 1939 Slessor published four books of verse; after the early 1940s he published no more poetry. In 1944, he published a collection titled *One Hundred Poems*, comprising all of his work which he wished to preserve. All but one of the poems I have reprinted in this selection are from that book. The exception is 'Streamer's End', which like the poem 'Wild Grapes' comes from *Backless Betty from Bondi*, a collection of light-verse sketches of female types from the Jazz Age and later.

At times almost in a spirit of *absit omen*, many have speculated about Slessor's early retirement from poetry-writing. Slessor himself gave differing but perhaps not irreconcilable reasons for his long silence, volunteering to his friend the novelist C.J. Koch that he didn't want to churn out 'little' poems, rather than real poems that needed to be written; on another occasion, he told me that 'if you can't change your style and rejuvenate it, you're finished with poetry.' During the long after-life of his writing, he was a benign influence in an admiring Australian literary world, never reviewing an author unless he could praise him but then praising most generously, giving impetus and imprimatur alike to many poetic careers. His physical presence is perhaps best caught by Vivian Smith, in the latter's poem 'Twenty Years of Sydney':

> That was the week I met Slessor alone
> walking down Phillip Street smoking his cigar,
> his pink scrubbed skin never touched by the sun.
> Fastidious, bow tie, he smiled like the Cheshire cat.
> 'If you change your city you are sure to change your style.'
> A kind man, he always praised the young.

Nuremberg

So quiet it was in that high, sun-steeped room,
So warm and still, that sometimes with the light
Through the great windows, bright with bottle-panes,
There'd float a chime from clock-jacks out of sight,
    Clapping iron mallets on green copper gongs.

But only in blown music from the town's
Quaint horologe could Time intrude ... you'd say
Clocks had been bolted out, the flux of years
Defied, and that high chamber sealed away
    From earthly change by some old alchemist.

And, oh, those thousand towers of Nuremberg
Flowering like leaden trees outside the panes:
Those gabled roofs with smoking cowls, and those
Encrusted spires of stone, those golden vanes
    On shining housetops paved with scarlet tiles!

And all day nine wrought-pewter manticores
Blinked from their spouting faucets, not five steps
Across the cobbled street, or, peering through
The rounds of glass, espied that sun-flushed room
    With Dürer graving at intaglios.

O happy nine, spouting your dew all day
In green-scaled rows of metal, whilst the town
Moves peacefully below in quiet joy. . . .
O happy gargoyles to be gazing down
    On Albrecht Dürer and his plates of iron!

Stars

'These are the floating berries of the night,
    They drop their harvest in dark alleys down,
    Softly far down on groves of Venus, or on a little town
Forgotten at the world's edge – and O, their light
Unlocks all closed things, eyes and mouths, and drifts
    Quietly over kisses in a golden rain,
Drowning their flight, till suddenly the Cyprian lifts
    Her small, white face to the moon, then hides again.

'They are the warm candles of beauty, hung in blessing on high,
    Poised like bright comrades on boughs of night above:
They are the link-boys of Queen Venus, running out of the sky,
    Spilling their friendly radiance on all her ways of love.

'Should the girl's eyes be lit with swimming fire,
   O do not kiss it away, it is a star, a star!'
   So cried the passionate poet to his great, romantic guitar.

But I was beating off the stars, gazing, not rhyming.
   I saw the bottomless, black cups of space
Between their clusters, and the planets climbing
   Dizzily in sick airs, and desired to hide my face.
But I could not escape those tunnels of nothingness,
   The cracks in the spinning Cross, nor hold my brain
From rushing for ever down that terrible lane,
   Infinity's trap-door, eternal and merciless.

The Ghost

'Bees of old Spanish wine
Pipe at this Inn tonight,
Music and candleshine
   Fill the dim chambers. . . .

'Fans toss and ladies pace,
Flutes of cold metal blow,
Maidens like winds of lace
   Tease the dark passages. . . .

'Run, you fat kitchen-boys,
Pasties in pyramids
Rise while your masters poise
   Flagons with silver lids. . . .

'Ha! Let the platters fume,
Jars wink and bottles drip,
Staining with smoke and spume
   Lips, tables, tapestries. . . .

'Wenches with tousled silk,
Mouths warm and bubble eyes,
Tumble those beds of milk
    Under carved canopies. . . .

'Now let your lovers dive
Deep to that hurricane. . . .
O, to be there alive,
    Breathing again!'

So the ghost cried, and pressed to the dark pane,
Like a white leaf, his face . . . in vain . . . in vain . . .

Next Turn

No pause! The buried pipes ring out,
    The flour-faced Antic runs from sight;
Now Colombine, with scarlet pout,
    Floats in the smoking moon of light.

Now programmes wave, heads bend between –
    The roaring Years go past in file.
Soon there's the Transformation Scene –
    And then the Footmen down the aisle.

For you must wait, before you leave
    This Theatre of Varieties,
Their frozen fingers on your sleeve,
    Their most respectful 'Now, sir, please!'

Out in the night, the Carriage stands,
    Plumed with black trees. The Post-boys grin.
The Coachman beats upon his hands.
    Turn after Turn goes on within.

The Night-Ride

Gas flaring on the yellow platform; voices running up and down;
Milk-tins in cold dented silver; half-awake I stare,
Pull up the blind, blink out – all sounds are drugged;
The slow blowing of passengers asleep;
Engines yawning; water in heavy drips;
Black, sinister travellers, lumbering up the station,
One moment in the window, hooked over bags;
Hurrying, unknown faces – boxes with strange labels –
All groping clumsily to mysterious ends,
Out of the gaslight, dragged by private Fates.
Their echoes die. The dark train shakes and plunges;
Bells cry out; the night-ride starts again.
Soon I shall look out into nothing but blackness,
Pale, windy fields. The old roar and knock of the rails
Melts in dull fury. Pull down the blind. Sleep. Sleep.
Nothing but grey, rushing rivers of bush outside.
Gaslight and milk-cans. Of Rapptown I recall nothing else.

from *The Atlas*

3   DUTCH SEACOAST

*('Toonneel der Steden van vereenighde Nederlanden met hare
Beschrijvingen uytgegeven by Joan. Blaeu.')*

No wind of Life may strike within
This little country's crystal bin,
Nor calendar compute the days
Tubed in their capsule of soft glaze.

Naked and rinsed, the bubble-clear
Canals of Amsterdam appear,
The blue-tiled turrets, china clocks
And glittering beaks of weathercocks.

A gulf of sweet and winking hoops
Whereon there ride 500 poops
With flying mouths and fleeting hair
Of saints hung up like candles there –

Fox-coloured mansions, lean and tall,
That burst in air but never fall,
Whose bolted shadows, row by row,
Float changeless on the stones below –

Sky full of ships, bay full of town,
A port of waters jellied brown:
Such is the world no tide may stir,
Sealed by the great cartographer.

O, could he but clap up like this
My decomposed metropolis,
Those other countries of the mind,
So tousled, dark and undefined!

Crow Country

Gutted of station, noise alone,
The crow's voice trembles down the sky
As if this nitrous flange of stone
Wept suddenly with such a cry;
As if the rock found lips to sigh,
The riven earth a mouth to moan;
But we that hear them, stumbling by,
Confuse their torments with our own.

Over the huge abraded rind,
Crow-countries graped with dung, we go,
Past gullies that no longer flow
And wells that nobody can find,
Lashed by the screaming of the crow,
Stabbed by the needles of the mind.

Elegy in a Botanic Gardens

The smell of birds' nests faintly burning
Is autumn. In the autumn I came
Where spring had used me better,
To the clear red pebbles and the men of stone
And foundered beetles, to the broken Meleager
And thousands of white circles drifting past,
Cold suns in water; even to the dead grove
Where we had kissed, to the Tristania tree
Where we had kissed so awkwardly,
Noted by swans with damp, accusing eyes,
All gone to-day; only the leaves remain,
Gaunt paddles ribbed with herringbones
Of watermelon-pink. Never before
Had I assented to the hateful name
Meryta Macrophylla, on a tin tag.
That was no time for botany. But now the schools,
The horticulturists, come forth
Triumphantly with Latin. So be it now,
Meryta Macrophylla, and the old house,
Ringed with black stone, no Georgian Headlong Hall
With glass-eye windows winking candles forth,
Stuffed with French horns, globes, air-pumps, telescopes
And Cupid in a wig, playing the flute,
But truly, and without escape,
THE NATIONAL HERBARIUM,
Repeated dryly in Roman capitals,
THE NATIONAL HERBARIUM.

Five Visions of Captain Cook

I

Cook was a captain of the Admiralty
When sea-captains had the evil eye,
Or should have, what with beating krakens off
And casting nativities of ships;
Cook was a captain of the powder-days
When captains, you might have said, if you had been
Fixed by their glittering stare, half-down the side,
Or gaping at them up companionways,
Were more like warlocks than a humble man –
And men were humble then who gazed at them,
Poor horn-eyed sailors, bullied by devils' fists
Of wind or water, or the want of both,
Childlike and trusting, filled with eager trust –
Cook was a captain of the sailing days
When sea-captains were kings like this,
Not cold executives of company-rules
Cracking their boilers for a dividend
Or bidding their engineers go wink
At bells and telegraphs, so plates would hold
Another pound. Those captains drove their ships
By their own blood, no laws of schoolbook steam,
Till yards were sprung, and masts went overboard –
Daemons in periwigs, doling magic out,
Who read fair alphabets in stars
Where humbler men found but a mess of sparks,
Who steered their crews by mysteries
And strange, half-dreadful sortilege with books,
Used medicines that only gods could know
The sense of, but sailors drank
In simple faith. That was the captain
Cook was when he came to the Coral Sea
And chose a passage into the dark.

How many mariners had made that choice
Paused on the brink of mystery! 'Choose now!'
The winds roared, blowing home, blowing home,
Over the Coral Sea. 'Choose now!' the trades
Cried once to Tasman, throwing him for choice
Their teeth or shoulders, and the Dutchman chose
The wind's way, turning north. 'Choose, Bougainville!'
The wind cried once, and Bougainville had heard
The voice of God, calling him prudently
Out of a dead lee shore, and chose the north.
The wind's way. So, too, Cook made choice,
Over the brink, into the devil's mouth,
With four months' food, and sailors wild with dreams
Of English beer, the smoking barns of home.
So Cook made choice, so Cook sailed westabout,
So men write poems in Australia.

II

Flowers turned to stone! Not all the botany
Of Joseph Banks, hung pensive in a porthole,
Could find the Latin for this loveliness,
Could put the Barrier Reef in a glass box
Tagged by the horrid Gorgon squint
Of horticulture. Stone turned to flowers
It seemed – you'd snap a crystal twig,
One petal even of the water-garden,
And have it dying like a cherry-bough.

They'd sailed all day outside a coral hedge,
And half the night. Cook sailed at night,
Let there be reefs a fathom from the keel
And empty charts. The sailors didn't ask,
Nor Joseph Banks. Who cared? It was the spell
Of Cook that lulled them, bade them turn below,
Kick off their sea-boots, puff themselves to sleep,

Though there were more shoals outside
Than teeth in a shark's head. Cook snored loudest himself.

One day, a morning of light airs and calms,
They slid towards a reef that would have knifed
Their boards to mash, and murdered every man.
So close it sucked them, one wave shook their keel,
The next blew past the coral. Three officers,
In gilt and buttons, languidly on deck
Pointed their sextants at the sun. One yawned,
One held a pencil, one put eye to lens:
Three very peaceful English mariners
Taking their sights for longitude.
I've never heard
Of sailors aching for the longitude
Of shipwrecks before or since. It was the spell
Of Cook did this, the phylacteries of Cook.
Men who ride broomsticks with a mesmerist
Mock the typhoon. So, too, it was with Cook.

III

Two chronometers the captain had,
One by Arnold that ran like mad,
One by Kendal in a walnut case,
Poor devoted creature with a hangdog face.

Arnold always hurried with a crazed click-click
Dancing over Greenwich like a lunatic,
Kendal panted faithfully his watch-dog beat,
Climbing out of Yesterday with sticky little feet.

Arnold choked with appetite to wolf up time,
Madly round the numerals his hands would climb,
His cogs rushed over and his wheels ran miles,
Dragging Captain Cook to the Sandwich Isles.

But Kendal dawdled in the tombstoned past,
With a sentimental prejudice to going fast,
And he thought very often of a haberdasher's door
And a yellow-haired boy who would knock no more.

All through the night-time, clock talked to clock,
In the captain's cabin, tock-tock-tock,
One ticked fast and one ticked slow,
And Time went over them a hundred years ago.

IV

Sometimes the god would fold his wings
And, stone of Caesar's turned to flesh,
Talk of the most important things
That serious-minded midshipmen could wish,

Of plantains, and the lack of rum
Or spearing sea-cows – things like this
That hungry schoolboys, five days dumb,
In jolly-boats are wonted to discuss.

What midshipman would pause to mourn
The sun that beat about his ears,
Or curse the tide, if he could horn
His fists by tugging on those lumbering oars?

Let rum-tanned mariners prefer
To hug the weather-side of yards;
'Cats to catch mice' before they purr,
Those were the captain's enigmatic words.

Here, in this jolly-boat they graced,
Were food and freedom, wind and storm,
While, fowling-piece across his waist,
Cook mapped the coast, with one eye cocked for game.

After the candles had gone out, and those
Who listened had gone out, and a last wave
Of chimney haloes caked their smoky rings
Like fish-scales on the ceiling, a Yellow Sea
Of swimming circles, the old man,
Old Captain-in-the-Corner, drank his rum
With friendly gestures to four chairs. They stood
Empty, still warm from haunches, with rubbed nails
And leather glazed, like agéd serving-men
Feeding a king's delight, the sticky, drugged
Sweet agony of habitual anecdotes.
But these, his chairs, could bear an old man's tongue,
Sleep when he slept, be flattering when he woke,
And wink to hear the same eternal name
From lips new-dipped in rum.

'Then Captain Cook,
I heard him, told them they could go
If so they chose, but he would get them back,
Dead or alive, he'd have them,'
The old man screeched, half-thinking to hear 'Cook!
Cook again! Cook! It's other cooks he'll need,
Cooks who can bake a dinner out of pence,
That's what he lives on, talks on, half-a-crown
A day, and sits there full of Cook.
Who'd do your cooking now, I'd like to ask,
If someone didn't grind her bones away?
But that's the truth, six children and half-a-crown
A day, and a man gone daft with Cook.'

That was his wife,
Elizabeth, a noble wife but brisk,
Who lived in a present full of kitchen-fumes
And had no past. He had not seen her
For seven years, being blind, and that of course

Was why he'd had to strike a deal with chairs,
Not knowing when those who chafed them had gone to sleep
Or stolen away. Darkness and empty chairs,
This was the port that Alexander Home
Had come to with his useless cutlass-wounds
And tales of Cook, and half-a-crown a day –
This was the creek he'd run his timbers to,
Where grateful countrymen repaid his wounds
At half-a-crown a day. Too good, too good,
This eloquent offering of birdcages
To gulls, and Greenwich Hospital to Cook,
Britannia's mission to the sea-fowl.

It was not blindness picked his flesh away,
Nor want of sight made penny-blank the eyes
Of Captain Home, but that he lived like this
In one place, and gazed elsewhere. His body moved
In Scotland, but his eyes were dazzle-full
Of skies and water farther round the world –
Air soaked with blue, so thick it dripped like snow
On spice-tree boughs, and water diamond-green,
Beaches wind-glittering with crumbs of gilt,
And birds more scarlet than a duchy's seal
That had come whistling long ago, and far
Away. His body had gone back,
Here it sat drinking rum in Berwickshire,
But not his eyes – they were left floating there
Half-round the earth, blinking at beaches milked
By suck-mouth tides, foaming with ropes of bubbles
And huge half-moons of surf. Thus it had been
When Cook was carried on a sailor's back,
Vengeance in a cocked hat, to claim his price,
A prince in barter for a longboat.
And then the trumpery springs of fate – a stone,
A musket-shot, a round of gunpowder,
And puzzled animals, killing they knew not what
Or why, but killing... the surge of goatish flanks

30

Armoured in feathers, like cruel birds:
Wild, childish faces, killing; a moment seen,
Marines with crimson coats and puffs of smoke
Toppling face-down; and a knife of English iron,
Forged aboard ship, that had been changed for pigs,
Given back to Cook between the shoulder-blades.
There he had dropped, and the old floundering sea,
The old, fumbling, witless lover-enemy,
Had taken his breath, last office of salt water.

Cook died. The body of Alexander Home
Flowed round the world and back again, with eyes
Marooned already, and came to English coasts,
The vague ancestral darknesses of home,
Seeing them faintly through a glass of gold,
Dim fog-shapes, ghosted like the ribs of trees
Against his blazing waters and blue air.
But soon they faded, and there was nothing left,
Only the sugar-cane and the wild granaries
Of sand, and palm-trees and the flying blood
Of cardinal-birds; and putting out one hand
Tremulously in the direction of the beach,
He felt a chair in Scotland. And sat down.

Wild Grapes

The old orchard, full of smoking air,
Full of sour marsh and broken boughs, is there,
But kept no more by vanished Mulligans,
Or Hartigans, long drowned in earth themselves,
Who gave this bitter fruit their care.

Here's where the cherries grew that birds forgot,
And apples bright as dogstars; now there is not
An apple or a cherry; only grapes,
But wild ones, Isabella grapes they're called,
Small, pointed, black, like boughs of musket-shot.

Eating their flesh, half-savage with black fur,
Acid and gipsy-sweet, I thought of her,
Isabella, the dead girl, who has lingered on
Defiantly when all have gone away,
In an old orchard where swallows never stir.

Isabella grapes, outlaws of a strange bough,
That in their harsh sweetness remind me somehow
Of dark hair swinging and silver pins,
A girl half-fierce, half-melting, as these grapes,
Kissed here – or killed here – but who remembers now?

Streamer's End

Roses all over the steamer,
    Paper all over the sky,
And You at the end of a streamer
    Smiling goodbye, goodbye.
It isn't to me you dangle,
    It isn't to me you smile,
But out of the rainbow tangle
    Our lines have crossed for a while.

Somebody's benediction
    Pitches a streamer – whizz! –
Under the firm conviction
    You're on the end of his.

Others may claim attention,
   Rolling away to sea,
But nobody's there to mention
   The cove at this end is ME!

Don't you consider the danger
   Of setting a heart on fire
By tossing a perfect stranger
   Your 10,000 volt live-wire?
I'm only a face on the skyline,
   Something the wharf obscures –
But you're on the end of my line,
   And I'm on the end of yours!

Off in the vast Orsova,
   Soon you will wave in vain;
I could be Casanova,
   You could be Queen of Spain –
I must go back to the city,
   You must go back to the King.
Blow me a kiss for pity,
   Girl at the end of the string!

Talbingo

'Talbingo River' – as one says of bones:
'Captain' or 'Commodore' that smelt gunpowder
In old engagements no one quite believes
Or understands. Talbingo had its blood
As they did, ran with waters huge and clear
Lopping down mountains,
Turning crags to banks.

Now it's a sort of aching valley,
Basalt shaggy with scales,
A funnel of tobacco-coloured clay,
Smoulders of puffed earth
And pebbles and shell-bodied flies
And water thickening to stone in pocks.

That's what we're like out here,
Beds of dried-up passions.

Waters

This Water, like a sky that no one uses,
Air turned to stone, ridden by stars and birds
No longer, but with clouds of crystal swimming,
I'll not forget, nor men can lose, though words
Dissolve with music, gradually dimming.
So let them die; whatever the mind loses,
Water remains, cables and bells remain,
Night comes, the sailors burn their riding-lamps,
And strangers, pitching on our graves their camps,
Will break through branches to the surf again.

Darkness comes down. The Harbour shakes its mane,
Glazed with a leaf of amber; lights appear
Like thieves too early, dropping their swag by night,
Red, gold and green, down trap-doors glassy-clear,
And lanterns over Pinchgut float with light
Where they so long have lain.
All this will last, but I who gaze must go
On water stranger and less clear, and melt
With flesh away; and stars that I have felt,
And loved, shall shine for eyes I do not know.

Country Towns

Country towns, with your willows and squares,
And farmers bouncing on barrel mares
To public-houses of yellow wood
With '1860' over their doors,
And that mysterious race of Hogans
Which always keeps General Stores....

At the School of Arts, a broadsheet lies
Sprayed with the sarcasm of flies:
'The Great Golightly Family
Of Entertainers Here Tonight' –
Dated a year and a half ago,
But left there, less from carelessness
Than from a wish to seem polite.

Verandas baked with musky sleep,
Mulberry faces dozing deep,
And dogs that lick the sunlight up
Like paste of gold – or, roused in vain
By far, mysterious buggy-wheels,
Lower their ears, and drowse again....

Country towns with your schooner bees,
And locusts burnt in the pepper-trees,
Drown me with syrups, arch your boughs,
Find me a bench, and let me snore,
Till, charged with ale and unconcern,
I'll think it's noon at half-past four!

A Bushranger

Jackey Jackey gallops on a horse like a swallow
Where the carbines bark and the blackboys hollo.
When the traps give chase (may the Devil take his power!)
He can ride ten miles in a quarter of an hour.

Take a horse and follow, and you'll hurt no feelings;
He can fly down waterfalls and jump through ceilings,
He can shoot off hats, for to have a bit of fun,
With a bulldog bigger than a buffalo-gun.

Honeyed and profound is his conversation
When he bails up Mails on Long Tom Station,
In a flyaway coat with a black cravat,
A snow-white collar and a cabbage-tree hat.

Flowers in his button-hole and pearls in his pocket,
He comes like a ghost and he goes like a rocket
With a lightfoot heel on a blood-mare's flank
And a bagful of notes from the Joint Stock Bank.

Many pretty ladies he could witch out of marriage,
Though he prig but a kiss in a bigwig's carriage;
For the cock of an eye or the lift of his reins,
They would run barefoot through Patrick's Plains.

The Nabob

(To the memory of William Hickey, Esq.)

Coming out of India with ten thousand a year
Exchanged for flesh and temper, a dry Faust
Whose devil barters with digestion, has he paid dear
For dipping his fingers in the Roc's valley?

Who knows? It's certain that he owns a rage,
A face like shark-skin, full of Yellow Jack,
And that unreckoning tyranny of age
That calls for turtles' eggs in Twickenham.

Sometimes, by moonlight, in a barge he'll float
Whilst hirelings blow their skulking flageolets,
Served by a Rajah in a golden coat
With pigeon pie . . . Madeira . . . and Madeira . . .

Or in his Bon de Paris with silver frogs
He rolls puff-bellied in an equipage,
Elegant chariot, through a gulf of fogs
To dine on dolphin-steak with Post-Captains.

Who knows? There are worse things than steak, perhaps,
Worse things than oyster-sauces and tureens
And worlds of provender like painted maps
Pricked out with ports of claret and pitchcocked eels,

And hubbubs of billiard-matches, burnt champagne,
Beautiful ladies 'of the establishment'
Always in tempers, or melting out again,
Bailiffs and Burgundy and writs of judgment –

Thus to inhabit huge, lugubrious halls
Damp with the steam of entrees, glazed with smoke,
Raw drinkling, greasy eating, bussing and brawls,
Drinking and eating and bursting into bed-chambers.

But, in the end, one says farewell to them;
And if he'd curse today – God damn your blood! –
Even his curses I'd not altogether condemn,
Not altogether scorn; and if phantoms ate –

Hickey, I'd say, sit down, pull up, set to:
Here's knife and fork, there's wine, and there's a barmaid.
Let us submerge ourselves in onion-soup,
Anything but this 'damned profession of writing'.

Toilet of a Dandy

Transports of filed nerves; a wistful cough;
One sensual hairbrush reluctantly concludes
The Great Harry's excruciations and beatitudes,
Delicately and gravely putting things on and off.

Shouting through shirts, dipping out liquid flowers,
All the accoutrements and mysteries,
The awful engines of the toilet – presses, trees,
And huge voluptuous bootjacks, for two shuddering hours.

But in the glass navel of his dressing-room,
Nests of diminishing mirrors, Narcissus peers,
Too nicely shined, parting the cracked, refracted sneers,
And meets the Corpse in Evening Dress; Caruso's tomb.

Metempsychosis

Suddenly to become John Benbow, walking down William Street
With a tin trunk and a five-pound note, looking for a place to eat,
And a peajacket the colour of a shark's behind
That a Jew might buy in the morning. . . .

To fry potatoes (God save us!) if you feel inclined,
Or to kiss the landlady's daughter, and no one mind,
In a peel-papered bedroom with a whistling jet
And a picture of the Holy Virgin. . . .

Wake in a shaggy bale of blankets with a fished-up cigarette,
Picking over 'Turfbird's Tattle' for a Saturday morning bet,
With a bottle in the wardrobe easy to reach
And a blast of onions from the landing. . . .

Tattooed with foreign ladies' tokens, a heart and dagger each,
In places that make the delicate female inquirer screech,
And over a chest smoky with gunpowder-blue –
Behold! – a mermaid piping through a coach-horn!

Banjo-playing, firing off guns, and other momentous things to do,
Such as blowing through peashooters at hawkers to improve the
    view –

Suddenly paid-off and forgotten in Woolloomooloo....

Suddenly to become John Benbow....

The Old Play

(... 'Madame, connaissez-vous cette vieille pièce? C'est une pièce
tout à fait distinguée, seulement un peu trop mélancolique.' –
H. Heine, *Tambour Legrand*.)

I

In an old play-house, in an old play,
In an old piece that has been done to death,
We dance, kind ladies, noble friends.
Observe our modishness, I pray,
What dignity the music lends.
Our sighs, no doubt, are only a doll's breath,
But gravely done – indeed, we're all devotion,
All pride and fury and pitiful elegance.
The importance of these antics, who may doubt?
Do you deny us the honour of emotion
Because another has danced this, our dance?
Let us jump it out.

II

In the old play-house, in the watery flare
Of gilt and candlesticks, in a dim pit
Furred with a powder of corroded plush,
Paint fallen from angels floating in mid-air,
The gods in languor sit.
Their talk they hush,
Their eyes' bright stony suction
Freezes to silence as we come
With our proud masks to act.
Who knows? Our poor induction
May take the ear, may still, perchance, distract.

Unspeakable tedium!
Is there nothing new in this old theatre, nothing new?
Are there no bristles left to prick
With monstrous tunes the music-box of flesh?
Hope dies away; the dance, absurd, antique,
Fatigues their monocles; the gods pursue
Their ageless colloquy afresh.

III

Marduk his jewelled finger flips
To greet a friend. Bald-headed, lean,
He wets his red transparent lips,
Taps his pince-nez, and gapes unseen.

Hequet to Mama Cocha cranes
Her horny beak. 'These fools who drink
Hemlock with love deserve their pains.
They're so convention, I think.'

Limply she ceases to employ
Her little ivory spying-lens.
'I much prefer the Egyptian boy
Who poisoned Thua in the fens.'

40

IV

But who are we to sneer,
Who are we to count the rhymes
Or the authorized postures of the heart
Filched from a dynasty of mimes?
Each has a part;

We do not hear
The mockers at our little, minion ardours,
Our darling hatreds and adulteries,
Our griefs and ecstasies,
Our festivals and murders.

And who are we, who are we,
That would despise the lawful ceremonies
Condoned by the coming of five Christs,
By the beating of an infinitude of breasts,
By Adam's tears, by the dead man's pennies,
Who are we?

V

And who are we to argue with our lutes,
How would we change the play?
Are we Lucifers with hell in our boots?
There are no Lucifers today.
By no means. It is never like this,
Never like this. One does not fall.
How should we find, like Lucifer, an abyss?
Never like that at all.

And who are we to pester Azrael,
Importunate for funeral plumes
And all the graces Death can sell –
Death in cocked feathers, Death in drawing-rooms,
Death with a sword-cane, stabbing down the stairs?

It is not like this at all,
Never, never like this.
Death is the humblest of affairs,
It is really incredibly small:
The dropping of a degree or less,
The tightening of a vein, such gradual things.
And then
How should we guess
The slow Capuan poison, the soft strings,
Of Death with leather jaws come tasting men?

VI

Camazotz and Anubis
Go no more to the *coulisses*.
Once they'd wait for hours,
Grateful for a few excuses,
Hiding their snouts in flowers,
Merely as a tribute to the Muses.

Those were the days of serenades.
Prima donnas and appointments.
Now they think longer of pomades,
Less of the heart and more of ointments.

Anubis dabbles with the world;
A charming man, perhaps a trifle sinister,
But with his stars on, and his tendrils curled,
Really, you'd take him for the Persian Minister.

But Camazotz has grown jaded
And likes an arm-chair in the stalls,
Being by brute necessity persuaded
That perfect love inevitably palls;
Such the divine adversity
Of passion twisting on its stem,
Seeking a vague and cloudier trophy
Beyond the usual diadem.

'More balconies! More lilac-trees!
Let us go out to the private bar.
I am so tired of young men like these,
Besides, I note he is carrying a guitar.'

VII

'Shang Ya! I want to be your friend' –
That was the fashion in our termitary,
In the gas-lit cellules of virtuous young men –
'Shang Ya! I want to be your friend.'
Often I think, if we had gone then
Waving the torches of demoniac theory,
We should have melted stone, astonished God,
Overturned kings, exalted scullions,
And ridden the hairy beast outside
Into our stables to be shod –
Such was the infection of our pride,
Almost a confederation of Napoleons.

> Though in Yuëh it is usual
>   To behead a cock and dog,
> Such was not considered binding
>   In our bloodless decalogue.
>
> But the tail-piece to the chapter
>   We so fierily began
> Resembled an old song-book
>   From the golden days of Han.

Ours was the Life-Parting
Which made the poets so elegantly tragic.
On and on, always on and on,
By fears and families, by a sudden plague of logic,
By an agreeable ossification,
By a thousand tiny particles of space
Widening the fissures of our brotherhood,
We were impelled from place to place,
Dismembered by necessitude.

Who could have called that soft, adhesive nag
We bounced our lives on, a wild horse?
We were given palfreys in the place of stallions;
As for the kings and scullions,
We should, no doubt, have brought them to our flag
Had we not forgotten the prescribed discourse.

On and on, driven by flabby whips,
To the Nine Lands, to the world's end,
We have been scattered by the sea-captains of ships,
Crying no more with bright and childish lips,
Even if we wanted to pretend,
'Shang Ya! Let me be your friend.'

VIII

This is really a Complete Life and Works,
The memorial of a great man
Who was born with Excalibur in his fist
And finished by asking questions.

Woken by a star falling on his tiles,
He rushed out, defying devils –
'Come forth, you monster!' Only neighbours peeped
Fish-eyed at this ferocity.

Repeatedly inviting the rogue to stand,
He hunted with a naked sword,
But though general admiration and sympathy were expressed,
The scoundrel was not detected.

At last, regrettable to state, he stopped.
Why honour a coward with pursuit?
So he began to use Excalibur in the kitchen,
Or on occasion as a hay-rake.

How did he know that Time at length would gnaw
The rascal's face with quicklime?
Gradually the print faded, a fog blew down,
He even forgot the nature of the outrage.

However, he managed to live very tolerably,
And now, in a substantial villa,
Having saved enough to purchase an annuity,
Is piously glad he never found anyone.

But Gutumdug and Vukub-Cakix,
Having already seen many great men,
May surely be pardoned if with foundered chins
They doze a little....

Phew...heu....
Doze a little.

IX

A bird sang in the jaws of night,
Like a star lost in space –
O, dauntless molecule to smite
With joy that giant face!

I heard you mock the lonely air,
The bitter dark, with song,
Waking again the old Despair
That had been dead so long,

That had been covered up with clay
And never talked about,
So none with bony claws could say
They'd dig my coffin out.

But you, with music clear and brave,
Have shamed the buried thing;
It rises dripping from the grave
And tries in vain to sing.

O, could the bleeding mouth reply,
The broken flesh but moan,
The tongues of skeletons would cry,
And Death push back his stone!

X

My strings I break, my breast I beat,
The immemorial tears repeat,
But Beli, yawning in the pit,
Is not at all impressed by it.

Fresh lachrymations to endure!
He champs a gilded comfiture –
'The song was stale five Acts ago;
Besides, it isn't Life, you know.'

XI

But Life we know, but Life we know,
Is full of visions and vertigo,
Full of God's blowpipes belching rubies forth,
And God's ambiguous grape-shot maiming saints,
Full of emancipations and restraints –
Thou poor, bewildered earth!

Thou givest us neither doom nor expiation,
Nor palm-trees bursting into praise;
Blow down thy fruit, we snatch our stomachful,
Thou turnest not thy gaze,
Knowing we do but rob a little time;
A flight of air; thou takest back the spoils.
O, for some thunder on our brother's crime,

Even a little harmless flagellation
Or a few miserable boils!

But thou! Thou dost not turn thy face
Either to buffet or explore.
The devils bask, the martyrs weep.
Art thou too proud in a high place,
Or too befuddled in thy sleep?
Art thou too languorous to roar?

XII

You that we raised
To the high places,
With painted eyes
And cloudy faces,
You that are named,
But no one finds,
Made out of nothing
By men's minds –
Be true to us,
Play us not false;
Be cruel, O Gods,
Not fabulous.

You were our statues
Cut from space,
Gorgon's eyes
And dragon's face;
Fail us not,
You that we made,
When the stars go out
And the suns fade.
You were our hope
Death to bless –
Leave us not crying
In emptiness.

The Knife

The plough that marks on Harley's field
   In flying earth its print
Throws up, like death itself concealed,
   A fang of rosy flint,

A flake of stone, by fingers hewed
   Whose buried bones are gone,
All gone, with fingers, hunters, food,
   But still the knife lives on.

And well I know, when bones are nought,
   The blade of stone survives –
I, too, from clods of aching thought,
   Have turned up sharper knives.

North Country

North Country, filled with gesturing wood,
With trees that fence, like archers' volleys,
The flanks of hidden valleys
Where nothing's left to hide

But verticals and perpendiculars,
Like rain gone wooden, fixed in falling,
Or fingers blindly feeling
For what nobody cares;

Or trunks of pewter, bangled by greedy death,
Stuck with black staghorns, quietly sucking,
And trees whose boughs go seeking,
And trees like broken teeth

With smoky antlers broken in the sky;
Or trunks that lie grotesquely rigid,
Like bodies blank and wretched
After a fool's battue,

As if they've secret ways of dying here
And secret places for their anguish
When boughs at last relinquish
Their clench of blowing air –

But this gaunt country, filled with mills and saws,
With butter-works and railway-stations
And public institutions,
And scornful rumps of cows,

North Country, filled with gesturing wood –
Timber's the end it gives to branches,
Cut off in cubic inches,
Dripping red with blood.

South Country

After the whey-faced anonymity
Of river-gums and scribbly-gums and bush,
After the rubbing and the hit of brush,
You come to the South Country

As if the argument of trees were done,
The doubts and quarrelling, the plots and pains,
All ended by these clear and gliding planes
Like an abrupt solution.

And over the flat earth of empty farms
The monstrous continent of air floats back
Coloured with rotting sunlight and the black,
Bruised flesh of thunderstorms:

Air arched, enormous, pounding the bony ridge,
Ditches and hutches, with a drench of light,
So huge, from such infinities of height,
You walk on the sky's beach

While even the dwindled hills are small and bare,
As if, rebellious, buried, pitiful,
Something below pushed up a knob of skull,
Feeling its way to air.

Vesper-Song of the Reverend Samuel Marsden

My cure of souls, my cage of brutes,
Go lick and learn at these my boots!
When tainted highways tear a hole,
I bid my cobbler welt the sole.
O, ye that wear the boots of Hell,
Shall I not welt a soul as well?
   O, souls that leak with holes of sin,
   Shall I not let God's leather in,
   Or hit with sacramental knout
   Your twice-convicted vileness out?

Lord, I have sung with ceaseless lips
A tinker's litany of whips,
Have graved another Testament
On backs bowed down and bodies bent.
My stripes of jewelled blood repeat
A scarlet Grace for holy meat.

Not mine, the Hand that writes the weal
On this, my vellum of puffed veal,
Not mine, the glory that endures,
But Yours, dear God, entirely Yours.

Are there not Saints in holier skies
Who have been scourged to Paradise?
O, Lord, when I have come to that,
Grant there may be a Heavenly Cat
With twice as many tails as here –
    And make me, God, Your Overseer.
    But if the veins of Saints be dead,
    Grant me a whip in Hell instead,
    Where blood is not so hard to fetch.

But I, Lord, am Your humble wretch.

Advice to Psychologists

You spies that pierce the mind with trenches,
    Feasting your eyes through private panes,
Who, not content with Heavenly stenches,
    Insist on taking up the drains,

For you I've only two suggestions,
    Who prowl with torches in this Bog –
Small good you'll get from asking questions;
    Walk on your nostrils, like a dog.

William Street

The red globes of light, the liquor-green,
The pulsing arrows and the running fire
Spilt on the stones, go deeper than a stream;
You find this ugly, I find it lovely.

Ghosts' trousers, like the dangle of hung men,
In pawnshop-windows, bumping knee by knee,
But none inside to suffer or condemn;
You find this ugly, I find it lovely.

Smells rich and rasping, smoke and fat and fish
And puffs of paraffin that crimp the nose,
Or grease that blesses onions with a hiss;
You find it ugly, I find it lovely.

The dips and molls, with flip and shiny gaze
(Death at their elbows, hunger at their heels)
Ranging the pavements of their pasturage;
You find it ugly, I find it lovely.

Cannibal Street

'Buy, who'll buy,' the pedlar sings,
'Bones of beggars, loins of kings,
Ribs of murder, haunch of hate,
And Beauty's head on a butcher's plate!'

Hook by hook, on steaming stalls,
The hero hangs, the harlot sprawls;
For Helen's flesh, in such a street,
Is only a kind of dearer meat.

'Buy, who'll buy,' the pedlar begs,
'Angel-wings and lady-legs,
Tender bits and dainty parts –
Buy, who'll buy my skewered hearts?'

Buy, who'll buy? The cleavers fall,
The dead men creak, the live men call,
And I (God save me) bargained there,
Paid my pennies and ate my share.

Full Orchestra

My words are the poor footmen of your pride,
Of what you cry, you trumpets, each to each
With mouths of air; my speech is the dog-speech
Of yours, the Roman tongue – but mine is tied
By harsher bridles, dumb with breath and bone.
Vainly it mocks the dingo strings, the stops,
The pear-tree flying in the flute, with drops
Of music, quenched and scattered by your own.

So serving-men, who run all night with wine,
And whet their ears, and crouch upon the floor,
Sigh broken words no man has heard before
Or since, but ravished in the candleshine,
Between the push and shutting of a door,
From the great table where their masters dine.

Five Bells

Time that is moved by little fidget wheels
Is not my Time, the flood that does not flow.
Between the double and the single bell
Of a ship's hour, between a round of bells
From the dark warship riding there below,
I have lived many lives, and this one life
Of Joe, long dead, who lives between five bells.

Deep and dissolving verticals of light
Ferry the falls of moonshine down. Five bells
Coldly rung out in a machine's voice. Night and water
Pour to one rip of darkness, the Harbour floats
In air, the Cross hangs upside-down in water.

Why do I think of you, dead man, why thieve
These profitless lodgings from the flukes of thought
Anchored in Time? You have gone from earth,
Gone even from the meaning of a name;
Yet something's there, yet something forms its lips
And hits and cries against the ports of space,
Beating their sides to make its fury heard.

Are you shouting at me, dead man, squeezing your face
In agonies of speech on speechless panes?
Cry louder, beat the windows, bawl your name!

But I hear nothing, nothing...only bells,
Five bells, the bumpkin calculus of Time.
Your echoes die, your voice is dowsed by Life,
There's not a mouth can fly the pygmy strait –
Nothing except the memory of some bones
Long shoved away, and sucked away, in mud;
And unimportant things you might have done,
Or once I thought you did; but you forgot,
And all have now forgotten – looks and words

54

And slops of beer; your coat with buttons off,
Your gaunt chin and pricked eye, and raging tales
Of Irish kings and English perfidy,
And dirtier perfidy of publicans
Groaning to God from Darlinghurst.

Five bells.

Then I saw the road, I heard the thunder
Tumble, and felt the talons of the rain
The night we came to Moorebank in slab-dark,
So dark you bore no body, had no face,
But a sheer voice that rattled out of air
(As now you'd cry if I could break the glass),
A voice that spoke beside me in the bush,
Loud for a breath or bitten off by wind,
Of Milton, melons, and the Rights of Man,
And blowing flutes, and how Tahitian girls
Are brown and angry-tongued, and Sydney girls
Are white and angry-tongued, or so you'd found.
But all I heard was words that didn't join
So Milton became melons, melons girls,
And fifty mouths, it seemed, were out that night,
And in each tree an Ear was bending down,
Or something had just run, gone behind grass,
When, blank and bone-white, like a maniac's thought,
The naphtha-flash of lightning slit the sky,
Knifing the dark with deathly photographs.
There's not so many with so poor a purse
Or fierce a need, must fare by night like that,
Five miles in darkness on a country track,
But when you do, that's what you think.

Five bells.

In Melbourne, your appetite had gone,
Your angers too; they had been leeched away
By the soft archery of summer rains
And the sponge-paws of wetness, the slow damp

That stuck the leaves of living, snailed the mind,
And showed your bones, that had been sharp with rage,
The sodden ecstasies of rectitude.
I thought of what you'd written in faint ink,
Your journal with the sawn-off lock, that stayed behind
With other things you left, all without use,
All without meaning now, except a sign
That someone had been living who now was dead:
'At Labassa. Room 6 x 8
On top of the tower; because of this, very dark
And cold in winter. Everything has been stowed
Into this room – 500 books all shapes
And colours, dealt across the floor
And over sills and on the laps of chairs;
Guns, photoes of many differant things
And differant curioes that I obtained. . . .'

In Sydney, by the spent aquarium-flare
Of penny gaslight on pink wallpaper,
We argued about blowing up the world,
But you were living backward, so each night
You crept a moment closer to the breast,
And they were living, all of them, those frames
And shapes of flesh that had perplexed your youth,
And most your father, the old man gone blind,
With fingers always round a fiddle's neck,
That graveyard mason whose fair monuments
And tablets cut with dreams of piety
Rest on the bosoms of a thousand men
Staked bone by bone, in quiet astonishment
At cargoes they had never thought to bear,
Those funeral-cakes of sweet and sculptured stone.

Where have you gone? The tide is over you,
The turn of midnight water's over you,
As Time is over you, and mystery,
And memory, the flood that does not flow.

You have no suburb, like those easier dead
In private berths of dissolution laid –
The tide goes over you, the waves ride over you
And let their shadows down like shining hair,
But they are Water; and the sea-pinks bend
Like lilies in your teeth, but they are Weed;
And you are only part of an Idea.
I felt the wet push its black thumb-balls in,
The night you died, I felt your eardrums crack,
And the short agony, the longer dream,
The Nothing that was neither long nor short;
But I was bound, and could not go that way,
But I was blind, and could not feel your hand.
If I could find an answer, could only find
Your meaning, or could say why you were here
Who now are gone, what purpose gave you breath
Or seized it back, might I not hear your voice?

I looked out of my window in the dark
At waves with diamond quills and combs of light
That arched their mackerel-backs and smacked the sand
In the moon's drench, that straight enormous glaze,
And ships far off asleep, and Harbour-buoys
Tossing their fireballs wearily each to each,
And tried to hear your voice, but all I heard
Was a boat's whistle, and the scraping squeal
Of seabirds' voices far away, and bells,
Five bells. Five bells coldly ringing out.

Five bells.

An Inscription for Dog River*

Our general was the greatest and bravest of generals.
For his deeds, look around you on this coast –
Here is his name cut next to Ashur-Bani-Pal's,
Nebuchadnezzar's and the Roman host;
And we, though our identities have been lost,
Lacking the validity of stone or metal,
We, too, are part of his memorial,
Having been put in for the cost,

Having bestowed on him all we had to give
In battles few can recollect,
Our strength, obedience and endurance,
Our wits, our bodies, our existence,
Even our descendants' right to live –
Having given him everything, in fact,
Except respect.

Beach Burial

Softly and humbly to the Gulf of Arabs
The convoys of dead sailors come;
At night they sway and wander in the waters far under,
But morning rolls them in the foam.

---

* 'At this point the hills approach the sea and rise high above the river; together they form a very serious obstacle which had to be negotiated by every army marching along the shore. Here the Egyptian Pharaohs therefore commemorated their successes, and their example was followed by all subsequent conquerors, Assyrian, Babylonian, Roman (and French) down to 1920.' – *Steimatsky's Guide to Syria and the Lebanon*. In 1942, General Sir Thomas Blamey had an inscription cut to celebrate the capture of Damour by Australian troops under his command.

Between the sob and clubbing of the gunfire
Someone, it seems, has time for this,
To pluck them from the shallows and bury them in burrows
And tread the sand upon their nakedness;

And each cross, the driven stake of tidewood,
Bears the last signature of men,
Written with such perplexity, with such bewildered pity,
The words choke as they begin –

'Unknown seaman' – the ghostly pencil
Wavers and fades, the purple drips,
The breath of the wet season has washed their inscriptions
As blue as drowned men's lips,

Dead seamen, gone in search of the same landfall,
Whether as enemies they fought,
Or fought with us, or neither; the sand joins them together,
Enlisted on the other front.

El Alamein.

Roland Robinson

Leonine of hair and carriage, devoted to his solitary muse as both strength and refuge, Roland Robinson wore the title of poet with uncomplicated antique dignity to the end of his long life. He was in no sense an intellectual poet of the university age, though he was welcome at universities, especially that of Newcastle. He was born of English parents in County Clare, and brought to Australia in 1921, when he was nine years old. By fourteen, he was already working, first as a houseboy on a sheep station in western New South Wales, then as a rouseabout (trainee general hand) and boundary rider. He was to have a host of occupations during his working life: horse trainer, jockey, fencer (the post-and-wire kind), builder, mill hand, railway fettler, artists' model, ballet dancer, gardener, catcher of snakes and crocodiles for a zoo, and in later life when supporting himself as a greenkeeper on a golf course he proudly used the title of agricultural labourer, in an echo of Robert Burns. His private life was at times tempestuous. It is related that a Freudian psychoanalyst once undertook an analysis of Robinson in order to uncover the roots of his poetic gift, and possibly the secret spring of poetry itself. After some months of an apparent collaboration of wizards, Robinson had visibly increased in health, vigor and even size, and the psychoanalyst, who had withered and become shaky, cried a halt to the research.

Roland Robinson was devoted to the poetry of Edward Thomas, and identified deeply with the minstrels and folk poets of all places and periods. At readings, he never read, but recited. He published eight volumes of verse in his lifetime, often containing the same poems, rewritten or not, and he collected and published five volumes of Aboriginal myths and legends. As well, he wrote a book of short stories about race relations in Australia and three volumes of autobiography. A natural radical, Robinson was influenced by the Communism of his time and by the decolonizing Jindyworobak school of Australian poets, which strove during the period from the mid-1930s to the 1950s to emphasize and to widen the indigenous resources of Australian culture. Integral to this project were an appreciation of Australian environment and inclusive borrowings from Aboriginal art. Robinson was ideally placed to benefit from both of these. Already interested in the native people before World War II, his service as a conscientious objector with the Civilian Construction Corps on railways in the Northern Territory brought him into contact with tribal Aborigines fully initiated in the Dreamings religion and practising its complex ritual.

Many of the poems Robinson published are admitted joint creations, renderings into verse of the traditions and the speech of, especially, semi-traditional elders of acculturated Aboriginal groups living in South Eastern Australia. So far as I know, all of these named figures actually existed. His earliest versions of mythic material were stilted and lofty, in the manner of earlier white poets, but he quickly arrived at a clear, limpid style for rendering more traditional legendary stories, and a respectful self-effacing way of reproducing the flavours of contact-English (now more pretentiously termed *kriol*) spoken by Aboriginal country-folk in settled regions. In both of these achievements, he is an important stylistic pioneer in Australian writing.

Drifting Dug-Out

Now that the fig lets fall her single stars
of flowers on these green waters I would be
withdrawn as Gul-ar-dar-ark the peaceful dove
sending his callings over the many springs,
over the fountains and the jets of song
of Nin the finch and Geek-keek the honeyeater.
I would be withdrawn as Gul-ar-dar-ark calling
out of the distant sky and tresses of the leaves,
now that the fig lets fall her single flowers
like stars to pass beyond my trailing hand.

And the Blacks are Gone

But this sea will not die, this sea that brims
beyond the grass-tree spears and the low, close scrub,
or lies at evening limitless after rain,
or breaks in languorous lines to the long golden beach

that the blacks called Gera, before the white man came.
And the blacks are gone, and I frighten the crimson-wing
and the wallaby in gullies where the rock-pools lie
fringed by acacias and stunted gums, and I come
out onto open ridges flowering before this sea.
And the blacks are gone, and we are not more than they,
tonight as I make my camp by the rain-stilled sea.

To a Mate

He was a man who, with his hand,
would make the language of the sand
that showed where piccaninny walked,
where emu trod or dingo stalked.

Euro's pad or writhe of snake,
or brolga's imprint he could make.
And he was one to booze and brawl
and lie beside the fire asprawl.

He was a man, when moved, who spoke
of how at Innaminka soak,
when the molten west grew dim,
the creatures from the desert's rim

came in to drink and play as he
lay watching by a hakea tree,
where stars and dingo howls, he swore
were solitude not known before.

Wherever now with swag outspread
he camps by soak or river-bed,
would that I saw his camp-fire's sparks
and hailed him through the paper-barks.

Would I might Find my Country

Would I might find my country as the blacks
come in and lean their spears up in the scrub,
and crouch and light their flickering fires and spread
their mission blankets on the ground beneath
the dark acacia and bauhinia trees.
Would I might find my people as the blacks
sit with their lubras, children, and tired dogs,
their dilly-bags, their bundles of belongings
tied up in scraps of some old coloured dress,
and pass the long straight smoking pipe around,
and talk in quiet calling voices while
the blood deep crimson flower of sunset burns
to smouldering ash and fume behind the trees,
behind the thin grassed ridges of their land.

Swift

Exhausted, this migrating bird
carried far southwards off its course,
lost to the constant streaming flight
of its companions' polar force;

swift, that emerging from cold rains,
passed on between two skies of stars,
failing towards the deep to find
branches to cling to: shrouds and spars;

spirit or derelict: mere hunched sweep
of wings that fold within the fire
of elemental storms that burns
blood, flesh, and sinew in desire,

identifies me, and I hold
to frozen ropes of those cross-trees:
a hunched sweep of mere pinions, bone,
spent on the dark antarctic seas.

The Swagman

Transfixed by stars, he lay upon the bed
he'd made inside the open siding-shed.
A locomotive came with monstrous roar,
a blinding light; then nailed boots on the floor.
Cramped and cold, he turned upon his side:
the stars were paling as the curlew cried.
Vivacious wagtail, lorikeet, thrush, and wren
woke him with song and it was daylight then.
He passed through grass where flowers hung like stars
and drove before him showers of budgerigars.
From distant ironbarks the currawongs' calls
told him of fern hung, shadowed mountain walls.
The huge sun bit him like a burning-glass:
swag up, he headed for the mountain pass.

Curracarang

A whip's crack wakes him. He feels the bed
of tea-tree branches he broke and spread
down when he came there. Now it is light
and the oval cave's mouth frames the white
sea, and the gully of Curracarang
where the wind, that all night howled and sang,
travels the tea-tree scrub and comes

silvering the banksias and the sapling gums.
All night he has slept there and the cave
has sheltered and kept him warm from the rave
of rain and wind that howled as it tore
at the break of branches. You shall be poor;
you shall lose faith, be desolate,
follow a star, that star curse your fate.
You shall lie down and with last breath
pray not to waken from that death.
From this despair, the wind cried in scorn,
shall your fierce exultation be born.
This he remembers the wind howled and sang
all night through the gully of Curracarang,
now that the whip-bird's tongue has uncurled
the shattering crack of its thong at the world.

Sundowner

Old sundowner, in shake-down overcoat,
under the store veranda staring
out at the rain. His pug-faced dog
shivers beside his battered suitcase.
– Who's the old man? I ask in the store
– Camps on the river, been routed out
by the rain.
        I drive off through the rain.
– Is it pity? It's ourselves we pity,
Ourselves we recognize and renounce.
I go back, make some remark on the rain,
pass him a hand-out. – Thanks, son. –

It's Langland lances me, though, as I leave:
Christ pursuing us in a poor man's apparel. –

The Prisoners

After our labouring train had passed
through those red sandridges at last
and, straightening out, went racing for
dark mountains in the desert's floor,
I saw, in that red-purple land,
the bearded Italian prisoners stand
beside the line until our train
should pass to let them toil again.
Then, clinging to the rushing car,
I leaned out, shouting: Come sta!
And, from blurred faces by the track,
heard: Bene! Bene! shouted back.
I looked and saw them where they stood
against those ridges red as blood,
looked and saw them lessen and
be lost in spinifex and sand.
There, we were carried northward while
my vision stayed and shared exile
with those men whom, I believed,
the blood deep desert had received.

The Ibis

Look! And the ibis, like a drifting smoke,
hung in the sky. And there the wind, that was
their purpose, swirled, distended them, and broke
their drift above the seas of red brown grass,

ribbed backbones of mountains, gleaming chains
of lilied billabongs fringed with reeds and trees
and, serpentine, through swamps and plains,
the rivers flowing to their different seas.

Drifting, in skeins and skeins, the ibis passed
far down the opal sky, where still I traced
their legend's poetry, until at last
from that oblivion it was quite effaced.

Deep Well

I am at Deep Well where the spirit trees
writhe in cool white limbs and budgerigar
green hair along the watercourse carved out
in deep red earth, a red dry course that goes
past the deep well, past the ruined stone
homestead where the wandering blacks make camp
(their campfire burning like a star at rest
among dark ruins of the fallen stone)
to find the spinifex and ochre red
sandhills of a land inhabited by those
tall dark tribesmen with long hair and voices
thin and far and, deepening, like a sea.
I am at Deep Well where the fettlers' car
travels towards the cool blue rising wave
that is the Ooraminna Range, and starts
those pure birds screaming from the scrub to swerve,
reveal their pristine blush in wings and breasts,
to scatter, settle and flower the desert-oak.
Here I have chosen to be a fettler, work
to lay the red-gum sleepers, line and spike
the rails with adze and hammer, shovel and bar,
to straighten up and find my mates, myself
lost in the spinifex flowing down in waves
to meet the shadow-sharpened range and know
myself grown lean and hard again with toil.
Here, in the valley camp where hills increase
in dark blue depths, the desert hakea stands
holding the restless finches and a single star.

I Had No Human Speech

I had no human speech. I heard
the quail-thrush cry out of the stones
and cry again its crystal word
out of the mountains' crumbling bones.

I had no human word, beyond
all words I knew the rush of ash-
grey wings that gloomed in one respond
storm-grey, to swerve, a crimson flash.

The speech that silence shapes, but keeps:
a ruin and the writhe of thin
ghost-gums against their rain-blue deeps
of night and ranges I drank in.

I lived where mountains moved and stood
round me. I saw their natures change,   ·
deepen and fire from mood to mood,
and found the kingfisher-blue range;

and found, where huge dark heliotrope
shadows pied a range's power,
mauve-purple at the foothill's slope,
the parakeelya, the desert-flower.

Yet, human, with unresting thought
tormented, turned away from these
presences, from converse sought
with deserts, flowers, stones, and trees.

The Tea-Tree and the Lyre-Bird

Hushed to inaudible sound the deepening rain
closed round me on those ridges where the road
had led me to hunger and darkness, and again
I heard its voice on leaves. I eased my load
against a rock and found the tea-tree flowering
out of the dark wet bush, and drew its spray
of close starred blossom over me with showering
of cold rain on my face. And when my way
led down through rocks, the lyre-bird halted me
with those full rich repeated notes that sprang
out of the darkness and the sound of rain, and he
was silent then but, as I waited, sang
again. Past roots and rocks I went along
rich with that flowering, rich with repeated song.

The Tank

Where once the grey scrub's finches cried with thin
voices through the heat their 'nin-nin-nin',
bursts now the golden burgeon of this change
before the gibber-plain, the pale blue range.
Here to the fettlers' sunken water-tank
the blacks came in. Their three dun camels sank
down on their knees. The tall and bearded blacks
unslung the water-drums tied to the packs,
filled them and called their camels, and were gone
to where, out on the iron plain, led on
their lubras, children, and lean dogs... to know
always the ranges' distant ebb and flow,
the wind-whorled sands that bare the parched white bone,
beneath their feet, the knife sharp gibber-stone.

The Whales

Dark traceries of tea-trees rise where stars
still burn the east. The low dark ridge appears
where honey-eaters' tremulous arias
awaken from the thrust of grass-tree spears.

Beneath the pelt of wallaby scrub the land
in sleeping forms of heave and hollow breathes
and, still unseen, by cliff and curve of sand
murmuring, the marbled deep recoils and wreathes.

I come where scrub in flower is like a lyre
set in the wind where sky and ocean meet.
The stars are done. The bars of cloud take fire,
and all the fretted coast lies at my feet.

O look! where, bursting from the swell of ocean
the whales arise and blow in bright commotion.

The Child Who Had No Father

Related by Fred Biggs

Before the white man came here
with his sheep,
the plains were covered with
all kinds of flowers.

Two sisters would go walking
at evening through
the flowers, looking for any
food they could find.

And when those sisters walked
among the flowers,
there were no mai, no men,
in all the world

One evening as one sister
walked along,
she saw one flower, and stooped,
and broke it off.

Inside, the flower looked like
a baby's face.
She got two bits of bark
and put the flower,

between them, underneath
a log. She thought
no more about it, and walked
on through the flowers.

Next evening this sister came
again. 'Oh, more
and more this flower has
a baby's face.'

She took some possum fur,
and wrapped it
round the flower, and laid it
beneath the log.

Next evening when this sister
came to find
the flower, she found a baby
sleeping there.

She found her breasts had milk
And every evening,
she went out through the flowers
and fed the child.

Her sister saw her sister's
breasts had formed
'Oh, you must have a baby,'
'Yes.' 'Oh, where?'

'Out there among the flowers'
The sisters went
and found the child and brought it
to their cave.

That child became a wise
and clever man
And, afterwards, he went up
into the sky.

And always, when I hear the
white men preaching
this story comes into
my mind. That child,

he was like Jesus, he came
into the world
without a father. He was
formed from a flower.

That woman touched that flower.
If she had not
plucked that flower, this could
not have happened.

The Fitzroy River Crossing

Camped above the Fitzroy River Crossing
under white limbed river-gums, I'm gathering
firewood this evening, walking through
graves and headstones lost in the dust and grass.
A red, protruding boulder is inscribed:
'James Lennon. Prospector. Died 14-9-08.'
I stand there with the firewood under my arm
and a voice is speaking to me out of the dust:
'It was wild country when first I came here.
I searched for gold. The Aborigines were wild.
They circled my camp, dragging their spears,
gripped between their toes, through the grass.
A black woman was my mate. She eased loneliness
and terrors. You who see the sun and stars,
hear the crescendos of the cockatoos, you wonder
at this grave and at that grave. You search for poetry.
Most search for wealth or love or fame;
leave children behind them that they may live on.
You, who stand listening to the whispered speech
of the dead, your words may be remembered, or forgotten.
You'll neither know nor care, as I do not now
care if ever I found gold or love or fame.'
It is a name, cut into a boulder. My campfire's
leaping and flowing on the wind. Summoned
out of the darkness, muscle rippling torsos fling
fork lightning limbs against the stars.
Turn in. Lie down. Those other sleepers will
not trouble you. Earth's deep blanket covers them
from the stars' cold blaze, the merciless suns.

The Star-Tribes

Related by Fred Biggs

Look, among the boughs. Those stars are men.
There's Ngintu, with his dogs, who guards the skins
of Everlasting Water in the sky.
And there's the Crow-man, carrying on his back
the wounded Hawk-man. There's the Serpent, Thurroo,
glistening in the leaves. There's Kapeetah,
the Moon-man, sitting in his mia-mia.

And there's those Seven Sisters, travelling
across the sky. They make the real cold frost.
You hear them when you're camped out on the plains.
They look down from the sky and see your fire
and, 'Mai, mai, mai!' they sing out as they run
across the sky. And, when you wake, you find
your swag, the camp, the plains all white with frost.

The Sleeping Bush

The chattering creek, the continual
shush of the distant waterfall
I heard when I looked out into the night.
Glint of fronds and blades in the light
of the moon, forms of crouching boulders,
the gums with their long hair over their shoulders,
I saw as I stood outside my tent
believing that night was almost spent.

No tenuous sound of the robin's song,
forerunner of all the myriad throng
of daybreak's birds, in the stillness stirred.
Only the water's sound I heard

as I stood there, wondering by what track
had I come, to find myself gone back
to a time and place, with the rocks and the trees
deep in the silent centuries.

The Cradle

A corrugated iron shack. One room.
Tree-posts its uprights, saplings, axe-
trimmed, its beams and rafters. It stands
fast, no matter how the huge hands
of mountain winds grasp it. Rain
is tumult, deafening peace on the roof.

Rain-forest rises behind it, a maze
of cicada-sound. Tonight you will hear
the creek like rain as, just on dark,
the cat-bird meows and yowls from the edge
of the jungle-forest. Your eyes will daze,
close in lamplight over your book.

The kettle sings on the 'Waratah' stove.
Pots and pans gleam on their ledge
above. You will wish dawn not to come.
You will sleep, a child, as the hoarse wind
cradles you in the trees, as the arm
of the mountain holds the light of the farm.

Communion

Listening, I lie and hear the rain come on,
steadily falling through the dark and cold:
it seemed far in a forest I had gone,
I made no sound upon the deep leaf-mould.
All round that forest rose sheer mountain walls,
day long I'd walked to reach that camping place,
hearing the sound of streams and waterfalls;
I stopped with the last sunlight on my face.
I stood and listened in that forest deep,
hearing the rain, the drip drip of the trees;
from this dark room communion now I keep:
there are no comrades as such thoughts as these.

The Two Sisters

Related by Manoowa

On the Island of the Spirits of the Dead,
one of two sisters talks.
'We must make a canoe and follow the way
the sun walks.'

They've filled the canoe with sacred
rannga things,
and paddled away into the night
singing ritual songs.

'Sister, look back!' the first sister calls.
'Do you see the morning star?'
Her sister looks out along their wake.
'Nothing. Nothing's there.'

The little sister has fallen asleep.
Again her sister calls,
'Sister, look back for the morning star.'
'Nothing. Nothing at all.'

A spear of light is thrown across
the sea and lies far
ahead upon the sister's course.
'Sister, the morning star.'

The sun comes up and walks the sky.
A fish with whiskers swims
ahead, and leaps out of the sea,
while the sisters sing.

Day and night, and day and night,
the sisters are gone
with the morning star and the leaping fish
and the sky-walking sun.

The sisters, hoar with dried salt spray,
the semen of the sea,
make landfall where parrots scream
from paperbark trees.

The sisters beach the bark canoe,
unload the *rannga* things.
They thrust one in the earth. From there
the first goanna comes.

They've gone inland. Their digging sticks
make sacred springs.
They leave behind them *rannga* forms
for all living things.

Out gathering food, the sisters have hung
their dilly-bags in a tree.
While they're away, men come and steal
their sacred ceremonies.

The sisters hear men singing and
song-sticks' 'tjong-tjong'.
'Cover your ears. We cannot hear
the sacred song.'

'O, all our sacred ceremonies
belong now to the men.
We must gather food, and bear
and rear children.'

Mapooram

Related by Fred Biggs

Go out and camp somewhere. You're lying down.
A wind comes, and you hear this 'Mapooram'.
'What's that?' you say. 'Why, that's a "Mapooram".'
You go and find that tree rubbing itself.
It makes all sorts of noises in the wind.
It might be like a sheep, or like a cat,
or like a baby crying, or someone calling,
a sort of whistling-calling, when the wind
comes and swings and rubs two boughs like that.

A Wirreengun, a clever-feller, sings
that tree. He hums a song, a 'Mapooram':
a song to close things up, or bring things out,
a song to bring a girl, a woman from that tree.
She's got long hair, it falls right down her back.
He's got her for himself. He'll keep her now.

One evening it was sort of rainy-dark.
They built a mia-mia, stripping bark.
You've been out in the bush sometime and seen
them old dry pines with loose bark coming off.
You get a lot of bark from them dry pines,
before they rot and go too far, you know.
That woman from the tree, she pulled that bark.
It tore off, up and up the tree. It pulled
her up into the tree, up, up into the sky.
Well, she was gone. That was the end of it.
No more that Wirreengun could call her back.

'Mapooram. Mapooram.' 'What's that?' you say.
Why, that's two tree boughs rubbing in the wind.

The Myth of the Mountain

Related by Eustan Williams

Look at that mountain Jalgumbun standing up,
see how it goes straight up on all its side.
No man can climb that mountain. Look at its head,
through the mist, covered with trees. I worked
as chainman to Phinney MacPherson, the surveyor
right along this range and, when we come
to Jalgumbun, he says to me, 'Now Eustan,
let me see them steps you say are cut
out in this mountain.' And as I pointed out
them steps, he stood there, writing in his notebook
the story of the mountain that I told him.

That mountain Jalgumbun was once a tree.
A man went after honey in that tree.
He climbed up with the vine-rope round himself

80

and round the tree. And as he climbed he cut
out footholds with his stone-axe. And his wives
were waiting in the forest down below.

'Where are you?' they called out. And he called back,
'I'm chopping out the honey.' Then these women
wanted to come up closer, but again
the man sang out, 'No, wait there where you are,'
and went on chopping, chopping out the honey.
At last he called out, 'Here it is,' and rolled
the piece of wood with all the honey in it
down to the butt and big roots of the tree.
They sat down in their camp and ate that honey,
and travelled then away along the range.

That night there was no moon. The women looked
out into the night and whispered together,
'Oh, look what is that "something" over there?'
'Oh, it's like a shadow.' 'See, that "something"
over there is blocking out the stars.'
And in the morning when they woke, they saw
the mountain that was never there before,
Jalgumbun standing up against the sky.

Well, there's a tree called Jalgumbun that grows
here in the ranges. It has a real soft skin.
The fellers from the mill at Urbenville
come with their axes, tractors, and their gear,
and fell and lop them trees and drag them
out from the ranges of their native home.

Billy Bamboo

Related by Billy Bamboo

This wild cherry tree makes good shade.
I lie down under it and go to sleep.
By and by I hear a big roaring sound.
'Oh, thunder storm coming up. I'll soon
fix him.' I break a branch off this tree
and burn it. The smoke goes straight up
into the sky. Those big rolling clouds
divide, one cloud goes one way, one cloud
the other way. You hear thunder rolling
down the sky.

         This is our sacred tree.
It belongs to all the blackfellers. You're a bit
of a blackfeller, you try it. You'll say
'That's true what old Billy Bamboo says.'

Well, my tribe got shot up. A white man found
a baby near the camp and took it back
to the station on his horse. That baby grew up
to be my father.

         A Victorian tribe fought
the Wallaga Lake tribe. An old man and his wife
were running away along a pad, carrying
a baby with them. Men with spears were hard
behind them. They saw a big log hollowed out
by fire. They put the baby inside the log
and ran on.

         A white man was riding his horse.
He heard a baby crying in the bush.
He came to the big log and listened.
He saw the pale feet of the baby sticking out.
He took the child and reared it and gave it
his name. And that baby was my mother.

Me? I'm Billy Bamboo. Anyone will tell you.
The buckjump rider, the bare knuckle fighter.
We used to stand toe to toe. We'd go down
to the creek and wash the blood off our faces
and come back and into it again. I was a flash
young feller in jodhpurs, riding boots and hat.

No, I can't see as well as I used to,
and I have to get about with this stick now.
You should have seen the old people. They would
have told you what the emu told the kangaroo.
Those old people are all gone from this mission.
They're all ghosts walking around in this place.

The Platypus

Related by Dick Donelly

Djanbun's the platypus. He was a man one time.
He came out of Washpool Creek, the old people said.
Djanbun's travelling, a firestick in his hand,
across the big mountains to the Clarence River.
He's blowing on the firestick to make it flame.
But it won't flame, and wherever the sparks
fall down from the firestick they turn to gold.

This platypus man's mouth starts to get wide
from blowing on the firestick. We used to blow
on the firestick when we were young. My mother
used to say to us, 'Don't blow on the firestick
like that, or you'll be like Djanbun the platypus.'

When Djanbun gets down to the Clarence River,
he's got a big mouth from blowing on the firestick.
He starts to wonder, 'What am I going to do now?'
He'd got tired of trying to make the firestick flame.
So he throws the firestick down, and he thinks,
'I'll jump into the water.' As soon as he jumps
in the water, he turns into a platypus. That's him,
that's Djanbun now. He was a man one time.

Now Billy Charlie, he found this nugget of gold
at the place where Djanbun jumped into the water.
When I heard about this, I thought, 'Well now,
that's the firestick he found.' Because he found
that gold where the firestick was thrown down.

The old people told me this story. They showed me
the way Djanbun went across the mountain range.

Captain Cook

Related by Percy Mumbulla

Tungeei, that was her native name.
She was a terrible tall woman
who lived at Ulladulla.
She had six husbands,
an' buried the lot.

She was over a hundred, easy,
when she died.
She was tellin' my father,
they were sittin' on the point
that was all wild scrub.

The big ship came and anchored
out at Snapper Island.
He put down a boat
an' rowed up the river
into Bateman's Bay.

He landed on the shore of the river,
the other side from where the
church is now.
When he landed he gave the Kurris clothes,
an' those big sea-biscuits.
Terrible hard biscuits they was.

When they were pullin' away to go back
to the ship, these wild Kurris
were runnin' out of the scrub.
They'd stripped right off again.
They were throwin' the clothes an' biscuits
back at Captain Cook
as his men were pullin' away in the boat.

The Bunyip

Related by Percy Mumbulla

Old Billy Poddam was a real bugeen, a clever
old-man. He used to have half-a-crown. He'd go
an' play cards, go through all his silver, an' then
he'd play his half-a-crown. He'd lose it, but
next day he'd have it back in his hand again.
No one could get that half-a-crown from him.

This old feller had a bunyip. It was his power,
his moodjingarl. This bunyip was high in front,
an' low at the back, like a hyena, like a lion.
It had a terrible big bull-head an' it was
milk-white. This bunyip could go down into the ground
an' take the old man with him. They could travel
under the ground. They could come out anywhere.
They could come out of that old tree over there.

Old Billy Poddam never did no harm to no one
all the time he was at Wallaga Lake.
He went out to Brungle, the home of his tribe,
an' did something wrong an' hurt his sister's feelings.
His sister caught him with the guneena stones.
She was as clever as he was. So, when he knew,
he caught his own sister with the guneena stones.
'Well,' he said, 'you'll die; I'll die too.'

That bunyip, he went away back to the swamp. If he
was comin' out of the swamp you'd see the water
bubblin' an' boilin'. He'd make the water all milky.

My old dad was smokin' his pipe by the chimney.
Mum heard this bunyip comin', roarin'. The ground
started to shake. He was comin' closer. He came
out of the ground underneath the tank-stand, he went
over to the chimney an' started rubbin' himself
against it. He started to get savage. He started to roar.
Mum told Dad to go out an' talk to him in the language.

Dad went out an' spoke to him in the language.
He talked to him, 'We are all right. No one
doing any harm. You can go away.' Dad followed him
across the road, talkin' to him in the language.

That's when I saw the bunyip. I looked out through
the window. He was milk-white. He had terrible eyes,
an' they were glarin' an' rollin' about. Every time
Dad spoke to him he'd roar. My old man was talkin',
'Everything is all right. Don't get savage here.'

The bunyip went down into the hill an' down into
the salt water. I've never seen that bunyip since.
It was the last people of the tribe who left him there.
He only shows himself to certain fellers.
You can hear him comin', pantin' 'Hah-hah-hah.'

He travels around, up an' down the coast
as far as Kempsey, lookin' for any one who has
done anything wrong. When he bites you, you die. He's
even been seen in Victoria, at Lake Tyers Mission.

The Frog Who Was a King
Related by Tom Whaddy, Gumbangirr Tribe

This happened at Grassy Heads. This happened when
the world was made, years and years ago.

There was an old-man, an old king he was.
He used to look after Australia, we'll say.
One day another old feller came from the other
side of the world. Where would he come from, Africa,
would he? That's where the lions and tigers are.

He came across to Grassy Heads and asked
the old king did he have any lions and tigers
in Australia. 'Yes,' said the old king,
'we've got all those things here.' He was telling
a lie. He didn't want those animals here.

Well, the old feller goes back to wherever he came
from. He came back with a tiger. That's deadly
isn't it? He asks the old king again. 'Have you
got anything like this here?' The old king says,
'Yoo, ngunee kunee walkung.' That means
'Yes, we've got all those things here.'

At last the old feller from the other side
got sick of bringing these animals over, he was
bringing them over one after another. So he cursed
the old king, 'Tsure ninga ngang yatanga!'

That means he turned the old king into a frog,
them big brown fellers. That big brown frog says,
'Wark, wark, wark. Ngunee kunee walkung. Gityeeng
boseeya.' This means, 'O, we don't want anything
like that. We've got 'em all here in this place.'

That old feller picked up the old king and threw him
down into a crevice in the rocks, and that's where
he is to this day. Because he told a lie.
But he saved Australia from those deadly animals.

So now we've got all the quiet animals, kangaroos,
emus, wallabies, possums, and all that – except the
crocodile. That old feller must have sneaked him in.

Trunk Line Call

Gull scream slashes wide open his sleep,
lashes him along his track winding way
round by the lake to 'phone, to shatter
her shuttered hurt. Is it self hurt only
can tell how headlong he stumbles, hurls

88

himself to humble himself? Daybreak,
coming fast, furious, burns above the far
forested shore; burns, turns the lake
cerise, salmon, turquoise. Its slender
she-oaks blacken, then shrivel, then melt
against that crucible's content. It cannot
last. It cannot outlast, outrange
his need. The coins drop. He hears her
voice: Love's need does not change.

Hairy Man

Moonrise. My footsteps on the road.
Forest furred, the mountain sleeps
under stars, the five ringed moon.
Mountains are mined, removed by Man;
the forests felled, fed to mills.
The Moon's the burnt out satellite
of Earth, stepping-stone for inter-
planetary Man. The myths? They began
in ignorance. Huge Hairy-Man who
haunts these mountains is reconciled.
Here then, under the mountain's height
count him out. I cannot. Thought
of him chills me. Large among leaves,
the Moon-Man's sitting in his mia-mia.

The Blue Gum Forest

Why do I stand here, stare about me?
Thirty years are gone since last
I clung, clambered, crashed down sheer
gorges' walls, found this forest.
Surely not merely in memory have I come
here. The blue gums soar, naked
smooth, to where they overarch and,
lost in height, mingle in myriad tongues.
How have I got here? Why do I stand,
long looking, long desiring, a fallen
trunk, lichened, mossed, host to ochre
red fungi, falling into mould at my feet?
I sink in pungent mould. Blue-grey
the pipes soar to their arches that lull,
linger, leave off, then swell, hail,
all hail in hosannas, in hosannas.

The Creek

You are one of those clear cold creeks
I found in my solitary, impetuous youth.
You are those innocent sonatinas running
from rock-shelf to pool to rock-shelf.
I make my camp beside you, a dove-grey
deep pool fretting its fronds and tangled
flowers. Waratahs burn above you. You
give me billyfuls of rainwater wine, a
bright wing-case, a boronia petal, a white
rose tinted tea-tree star. I thought all
my creeks were spent, shrivelled at their
source, that time had stamped out my last
campfire, that never again should I kindle

ritual incense, my prayers, psalms. Now
by your plashing pool, needle sharp near,
rings the rain wrought round of the wren.
You are that image which had never died
in me, Eve, of my primavera, personified.

Northern Oriole

The tumult ends, the downpour stops.
On broad palm leaves the large warm drops
cling. That bird calls out again
as though his throat were filled with rain.
From tree to tree he glides among
the dripping leaves and makes his song.
Now from the poinciana's bough
sounds his echoing song, and now
deep within the banyan's shade,
that bell like, flute cool call is made.
High in the orange flowering gum
his voice is heard, but where I come
he makes no more that blended note
as though the rain had filled his throat.
Swooping, with folded wings he goes
over the far tree tops for those
mountains of the clouds and where
the storms let down their purple hair.

David Campbell

David Campbell was quintessentially a man of the Monaro, that high pastoral upland of hot dry summers and bitter winters that lies to the south west of Sydney. He was tuned to its dry enormous light, its racy legpulling traditions and its often patrician manners. Changes in ideology and the patterns of privilege in Australia mean that it is doubtful any man will ever again live so perfect a paradigm of the squatter (landed gentry) life, and certainly none will live it with the same gusto and aplomb. From birth on Ellerslie station near Adelong and captaincy of the King's School at Parramatta he moved to Arts and a rugby blue at Cambridge and two international caps playing rugby for England in 1937. Marriage and service in the Royal Australian Air Force followed, and he rose to the rank of Wing Commander, winning two Distinguished Flying Crosses for bravery in the air. After the war, he farmed on Palerang and Wells stations outside Canberra, where his three children were born. Divorced and remarried, he moved to a smaller property named Folly Run on the upper Molonglo river. Following outspoken opposition to the Vietnam war in the 1960s, he took an active part in the efflorescence of poetry in the national capital that lasted into the early 1980s. However, the accidental death of his beloved only daughter in the mid-1970s devastated him, and he died of lung cancer in the winter of 1979.

The poetic traditions that first attracted Campbell were the cavalier ones: he took with him from the bush a great love of the Australian ballad and at Cambridge his eyes were opened to the Metaphysicals and to W.B. Yeats. Under the influence of his friend the Australian poet and KGB operative John Manifold, who had also come to Cambridge from a squatter background, Campbell also read in other poetries, notably Spanish and border Scots, and while at the University he wrote and published his first poems to considerable praise. His first collection, *Speak with the Sun*, was published in England in 1949, and several more followed in Australia, especially from the 1960s onward, when a second large spurt of writing was accompanied by a broadening of his subject matter and a move into blank and free verse. In contrast to the majority of poets, he was most experimental not in his first period but his last.

Harry Pearce

I sat beside the red stock route
And chewed a blade of bitter grass
And saw in mirage on the plain
A bullock wagon pass.
Old Harry Pearce was with his team.
'The flies are bad,' I said to him.

The leaders felt his whip. It did
Me good to hear old Harry swear,
And in the heat of noon it seemed
His bullocks walked on air.
Suspended in the amber sky
They hauled the wool to Gundagai.

He walked in Time across the plain,
An old man walking in the air;
For years he wandered in my brain,
And now he lodges here.
And he may drive his cattle still
When Time with us has had his will.

Men in Green

There were fifteen men in green,
Each with a tommy-gun,
Who leapt into my plane at dawn;
We rose to meet the sun.

Our course lay to the east. We climbed
Into the break of day,
Until the jungle far beneath
Like a giant fossil lay.

We climbed towards the distant range
Where two white paws of cloud
Clutched at the shoulders of the pass.
The green men laughed aloud.

They did not fear the ape-like cloud
That climbed the mountain crest
And rode the currents of the air
And hid the pass in mist.

They did not fear the summer's sun
In whose hot centre lie
A hundred hissing cannon shells
For the unwatchful eye.

And when at Dobadura we
Set down, each turned to raise
His thumb towards the open sky
In mockery and praise.

But fifteen men in jungle green
Rose from the kunai grass
To come aboard, and my green men
In silence watched them pass:
It seemed they looked upon themselves
In a prophetic glass.

There were some leaned on a stick
And some on stretchers lay,
But few walked on their own two feet
In the early green of day.

They had not feared the ape-like cloud
That climbed the mountain crest;
They had not feared the summer's sun
With bullets for their breast.

Their eyes were bright, their looks were dull,
Their skin had turned to clay.
Nature had met them in the night
And stalked them in the day.

And I think still of men in green
On the Soputa track
With fifteen spitting tommy-guns
To keep a jungle back.

The Stockman

The sun was in the summer grass,
The coolibahs were twisted steel:
The stockman paused beneath their shade
And sat upon his heel,
And with the reins looped through his arm
He rolled tobacco in his palm.

His horse stood still. His cattle dog
Tongued in the shadow of the tree,
And for a moment on the plain
Time waited for the three.
And then the stockman licked his fag
And Time took up his solar swag.

I saw the stockman mount and ride
Across the mirage on the plain;
And still that timeless moment brought
Fresh ripples to my brain:
It seemed in that distorting air
I saw his grandson sitting there.

Winter Stock Route

Here where red dust rose
To raddle sheep and men
And the kelpie tongued at noon,
Silence has come again.
The great-boled gumtrees bow
Beneath their load of snow.

The drover and his dray
Have gone; and on this hill
I find myself alone
And Time standing still.
Printless the white road lies
Before my quiet skis.

But where my skis trace
Their transient snow furrow,
For generations both
Man and beast will follow.
Now in this winter passage
I cross the deserted stage.

Small-town Gladys

There are rows of bottles against the glass;
I look between and my air's blonde grass,
My lips are berries and my skin is cream
And I fill my frock to the very brim
And twirl a curl when the sportsmen pass –
And I'm a good girl, I am.

They call me Glad and say I'm a queen.
I look in the glass and my eyes are green
And they talk to men though they make no sound
For it's love that makes the world go round;
But go too far and I say, 'Go on;
I am a good girl, I am.'

In every novel I'm Lady Jane,
I use the book as a wicked fan,
And I sit on a stool and my fingers knit
A web to snare a sportsman's wit;
And they look at me as they look for rain,
But I'm a good girl, I am.

Under the willows, under the night,
Where schoolboys spy and the parson might,
I am the moon that rules the tides
Of men. And I shake and hold my sides
And I say, 'My make-up's an awful sight –
And I'm a good girl, I am.'

Winter

When magpies sing in sky and tree
And colts like dragons snuff the air
And frosts paint hollows white till three
And lamp-lit children skip their prayer;
Then Meg and Joan at midnight lie
And quake to hear the dingoes cry
Who nightly round the white church stone
Snap at their tails and the frosty moon.

When stockmen lapped in oilskins go
And lambing ewes on hill-tops bleat
And crows are out and rain winds blow
And kettles simmer at the grate;
Then Meg and Joan at midnight lie
And quake to hear the dingoes cry
Who nightly round the white church stone
Snap at their tails and the weeping moon.

Soldier's Song

Though I march until I drop
And my bed is sand,
I have filled the desert's cup,
Harvested its land;
And this I learned from the desert wind,
From the sphinx it blows:
The Murray's source is in the mind
And at a word it flows.

Though I climb the bitter rock,
Jungle for a bed,
I can muster such a flock
As never Falkiner bred;
And this I learned from the tropic wind
Where the giant storm grows:
The Murray's source is in the mind
And at a word it flows.

Windy Gap

As I was going through Windy Gap
A hawk and a cloud hung over the map.

The land lay bare and the wind blew loud
And the hawk cried out from the heart of the cloud,

'Before I fold my wings in sleep
I'll pick the bones of your travelling sheep,

'For the leaves blow back and the wintry sun
Shows the tree's white skeleton.'

A magpie sat in the tree's high top
Singing a song on Windy Gap

That streamed far down to the plain below
Like a shaft of light from a high window.

From the bending tree he sang aloud,
And the sun shone out of the heart of the cloud

And it seemed to me as we travelled through
That my sheep were the notes that trumpet blew.

And so I sing this song of praise
For travelling sheep and blowing days.

Here's to Sydney

Here's to Sydney by the summer!
Body-surfing down a comber
Where the girls are three a gallon
To a beach of yellow pollen;

Breaking hearts and backing horses
(Bookies weeping in their purses,
Licking thumbs and counting tenners);
Dreaming up tomorrow's winners;

Paris maids when I awaken
Serving Moet with the bacon
Lying round on leopard-skins
With brides and broads and mannequins;

Frowning at vice-regal balls –
Kiss my aunt and Tattersall's!
Tattersall's, I am thy farrow,
Keep a place for me tomorrow.

So the gentle presser sang
While the cutout whistle rang; –
And Lady do not question why
He lies dead drunk in Gundagai.

Six Centuries of Poetry

To open up this lofty theme
Let's take a couple making love
In a tall pear-tree – Chaucer's scheme
For pinning young men's hearts above
Their pockets. See, she strains to him
And the spring day is quite enough
For mistress and for page although
A tethered husband chafes below.

Yeats walked on stilts for forty years
And lay down in a woman's mind
Yet wondered at the bitter pears
And why her mouth was full of wind,
Till catching skirts to block his ears
He found a girl with less defined
Ideas, and in the dawn his song
And she cried in their natural tongue.

To the Art of Edgar Degas

Beachcomber on the shores of tears
Limning the gestures of defeat
In dancers, whores and opera-stars –
The lonely, lighted, various street

You sauntered through, oblique, perverse,
In your home territory a spy,
Accosted you and with a curse
You froze it with your Gorgon's eye.

With what tense patience you refine
The everyness of everyday
And with free colour and a line
Make mysteries of flaccid clay!

By what strange enterprise you live!
Edgy, insatiably alone,
You choose your tenderness to give
To showgirls whom you turn to stone –

But stone that moves, tired stone that leans
To ease involuntarily the toe
Of ballet-girls like watering-cans
(Those arguers at the bar) as though

In their brief pause you found relief
From posed dilemmas of the mind –
Your grudging aristocratic grief,
The wildcat cares of going blind.

Well, walk your evening streets and look
Each last eleven at the show:
The darkening pleasures you forsook
Look back like burning windows now.

Hear the Bird of Day

Hear, the bird of day
Stirs in his blue tree,
Fumbles for words to say
The things a bird may learn
From brooding half the night,
What's matter but a hardening of the light?

Out of this seed of song
Discoursing with the dark,
Now in a clear tongue
Rises his lonely voice,
And all the east is bright.
What's matter but a hardening of the light?

Mountain and brilliant bird,
The ram and the wren,
For each there is a word;
In every grain of sand
Stands a singer in white.
What's matter but a hardening of the light?

Windy Nights

Naked in snowdrifts, we've made love,
In city parks, at the front gate,
And thought no deeper truth to prove
Than this, that lovers cannot wait.
What if the whole world disapprove,
Though it should be a crowded street?
See how instinctive lovers move
To get their clothes off when they meet.
O what do lovers love the best,
Upstairs naked or downstairs dressed?
Windy nights and hot desire
Or an old book and a steady fire?
Ask your mistress. Should she pause,
She has a lover out of doors.

A Song and a Dance

The lean man of the desert speaks:
Your hearts are stale from greed and care.
O come out in the desert air
And wash your hearts in the desert creeks
For love comes when the heart is bare.
We piped to you, but you did not dance;
We sang you dirges, you did not weep.

Another came with wine and bread
And sat down with a prostitute,
For she loved much though her sins were great.
Come eat and drink with us, he said,
For the tree is known by its fruit.
We piped to you, but you did not dance;
We sang you dirges, you did not weep.

For a dancing girl they lopped one's head,
And nailed the other to a tree,
And laughed till the tears ran down, For we
May tell this tree by its fruit, they said,
And give the lie to his mockery,
We piped to you, but you did not dance;
We sang you dirges, you did not weep.

Song for the Cattle

Down the red stock route
Hock-deep in mirage
Rode the three black drovers
Singing to the cattle.

And with them a young woman,
Perhaps some squatter's daughter
From homestead or township,
Who turned her horse easily.

To my mind she was as beautiful
As the barmaid in Brewarrina
Who works at the Royal. Men
Ride all day to see her.

Fine-boned as a brigalow
Yet ample as a granary,
She has teeth good for laughing
Or biting an apple.

I'm thinking of quitting
My mountain selection,
The milking at morning
And the lonely axe-echoes;

Of swapping my slab hut
For a rolled-up blanket
And heading north-westward
For a life in the saddle –

For the big mobs trailing
Down the empty stock routes,
A horned moon at evening
And songs round the campfire.

Yes, I'll soon be drinking
At the Royal in Brewarrina
And ambling through mirage
With the squatter's daughter.

Mothers and Daughters

The cruel girls we loved
Are over forty,
Their subtle daughters
Have stolen their beauty;

And with a blue stare
Of cool surprise,
They mock their anxious mothers
With their mothers' eyes.

Chansons Populaires

Qui belles amours a, souvent si les remue

I

Hey Jack, give the grog and the women a rest.
I'm ambling through Goulburn as cool as a trout
Though the chestnut is bucking and titting about
(Hey Jack! give the grog and the women a rest!)

When who should I see all dolled-up in her best
But Rose from the Royal and just stepping out
With this woolbuyer toff, so I give him a shout,
Hey Jack, give the grog and the women a rest!

Well, his look would freeze Bourke but I see she's impressed
So I reins to the kerb and I holds an arm out
And she's up! and we settles for oysters and stout.
Hey Jack, give the grog and the women a rest!

Soldier Settlers

They hunt the standing green from sun-up for
Good stringybark for splitting. On the breeze
All day you'll hear, eating at hush, the wheeze
And tanged complaining of a crosscut or
The yelping of their axes. How they gnaw
At silence in the bellies of the trees!
And when high-up she shudders, from spread knees
They leap to watch green timber thump the floor
As if the sky keeled over. Then cleanly they
Lop head and branch and with iron wedges clout
The trunk to fence-posts. They can cut and lay
Ten miles of posts a fortnight. But the drought!
It eats into them – wire won't keep it out –
And has downed handier battlers in its day.

Old Age of an Old Dog

A kitten aids old Peter on his round
Of pines. The urgent cyphers jetted on
Their butts and pockets hollowed out of sun
Are canine, for a kitten too profound
That flirts a tail and scarves herself around
Peter who would rather be alone
And if he could would warn the kitten, 'Son,
Did not your mother tell you of the *hound*?'
Time was the station tongued his every move
And drover dogs, confronted, large with hair,
Recalling prior engagements would remove
Themselves with lightfoot negligence from where
The mogul glowered with bitch and bone to spare
Who must in age be satisfied with love.

The Australian Dream

The doorbell buzzed. It was past three o'clock.
The steeple-of-Saint-Andrew's weathercock
Cried silently to darkness, and my head
Was bronze with claret as I rolled from bed
To ricochet from furniture. Light! Light
Blinded the stairs, the hatstand sprang upright,
I fumbled with the lock, and on the porch
Stood the Royal Family with a wavering torch.

'We hope,' the Queen said, 'we do not intrude.
The pubs were full, most of our subjects rude.
We came before our time. It seems the Queen's
Command brings only, "Tell the dead marines!"
We've come to you.' I must admit I'd half
Expected just this visit. With a laugh
That put them at their ease, I bowed my head.
'Your Majesty is most welcome here,' I said.
'My home is yours. There is a little bed
Downstairs, a boiler-room, might suit the Duke.'

He thanked me gravely for it and he took
Himself off with a wave. 'Then the Queen Mother?
She'd best bed down with you. There is no other
But my wide bed. I'll curl up in a chair.'
The Queen looked thoughtful. She brushed out her hair
And folded up *The Garter* on a pouf.
'Distress was the first commoner, and as proof
That queens bow to the times,' she said, 'we three
Shall share the double bed. Please follow me.'

I waited for the ladies to undress –
A sense of fitness, even in distress,
Is always with me. They had tucked away
Their state robes in the lowboy; gold crowns lay
Upon the bedside tables; ropes of pearls

Lassoed the plastic lampshade; their soft curls
Were spread out on the pillows and they smiled.
'Hop in,' said the Queen Mother. In I piled
Between them to lie like a stick of wood.
I couldn't find a thing to say. My blood
Beat, but like rollers at the ebb of tide.
'I hope your Majesties sleep well,' I lied.
A hand touched mine and the Queen said, 'I am
Most grateful to you, Jock. Please call me Ma'am.'

Hotel Marine

Lost in glass gullies, searching for a suitcase:
The white sun shatters in ten thousand windows,
And splinters scatter, colouring the crowd
Looking for the Hotel Marine.

Our books are there, small treasures, a transistor
And all our marvellous clothes. I guess that's why
We wander naked through the rush-hour traffic
Looking for the Hotel Marine.

We use our hands as shields but no one sees us
In this steel garden with its paper leaves.
Their eyes are twenty blocks or hours before them
Looking for the Hotel Marine.

We keep together, eyes wide for a policeman,
But no one cares. Perhaps they are not here
But somewhere in the past or in the future
Looking for the Hotel Marine.

Maybe it's round the corner, sunlit, floating;
The doorman smiles and cats are on the sofas –
How should it vanish, leaving us with nothing,
Looking for the Hotel Marine?

Ku-ring-gai Rock Carvings

I

THE LOVERS

Making love for ten thousand years on a rockledge:
    The boronia springs up purple
  From the stone, and we lay together briefly
  For as long as those two lovers.

HONEYEATERS

The gymea and emus wait for the lithe tribesmen
    And the great whales doze, but the fish
  Leap down the flowering sandstone
  Where honeyeater chickens rage.

FISH

Trapped on a blue hill above blue bays
    The stone shoals move one way:
  From rockledge through the blue heads,
  It is light-years to the open sea.

MAN AND WOMAN

All night they look at the moon. No one sees them move,
    Though his arms are raised in praise.
  Delicately their ankles cross
  And her fork is an inch-deep groove.

WHALES

They whistled the whales and whales litter the landscape
    Like stranded boulders with calves
  Carved on their backs. And there they blow
  Low banksia scrub, a froth of spiked spring flowers.

SPRING

The Chase is mad with sex. Flowered trees sustain
        The act of love a season;
    While from stone loins wild orchids spring
    Whose pleasure is in intercourse with beetles.

SPINY ANT-EATERS

Spring comes in gold and purple, and the stone echidnas
        Dawdle across the rockface:
    It may be a prickly business
    But their desire goes on forever.

FAIRY PENGUINS

A fairy penguin dives in rock for cover
        With swept-back wings, as jets
    Pencilling vapour-trails, go over:
    For all I know, the rest may still be under.

II

LIZARDS

Lizards are kin and can return to stone
        At will. Transfixing a shield
    Like a spear a lizard froze in the sun, a thing
    Of bronze, yet quick. See the dart of his tongue!

BORA RING

The kangaroo has a spear in his side. It was here
        Young men were initiated,
    Tied to a burning tree. Today
    Where are such cooling pools of water?

TENCH, 1791

Flesh carvings: for theft, before the assembled tribes,
*   A convict was flogged. Daringa,*
*   Her nets forgotten, wept: while Barangaroo*
*   Threatened the lasher. A feckless if tender people.*

KING BOONGARIE: ETCHING BY EARLE

A convict driving nails in a deal coffin:
    They're burying the tribe's last king
    Beside Queen Gooseberry with naval honours.
    His Commodore's uniform (Brisbane's) is in tatters.

RAIN

The waterfalls are real. All night it rained
    On black rock where eels
    Slither and cling for centuries
    Out there in the black hills.

SHIELDS

A shield was the symbol of the tribe rather than the spear
    Or boomerang. In caves
    And on tessellated pavements, shields
    Forbid the stranger, but hearth and heart are bare.

WEAPONS

In 'the war to end all wars', an obsolete tank
    Patrolling the blue littoral
    From Gabo to York, pitted the rock
    And unearthed from moss a boomerang.

FIRE

Ladyslippers tiptoe to the carved birds
    Where the great fire blazed
    Last summer. After the corroboree of flame,
    Black crows complained of two lyrebirds dancing.

III

THE UNDERGROUND

The underground is stirring. Orchid and bird
    Rise from the ashes, seed
  Spread beetle wings; and August's student tribes
  Step out between the blackened trees.

CHARCOAL DRAWINGS

We drew in charcoal by the poisoned water
    And you cried, Look, a sunfish!
  Light wrinkled stone but you had gone
  Like a blue crane in blue creekwater.

LYREBIRDS

The lyrebird is a de Berg. She records
    The sound of men and of birds.
  The Ku-ring-gal live in their rock carvings
  And a note or two of the lyrebird.

HANDS

An artist blew ruddy ochre to outline his hand
    In a cave the water glazed.
  You can shake hands with this dead man.
  It teases the mind like John Keats' hand.

WOOLGATHERING

The white-eared honeyeater is fixed in time
    By the hand of Douglas Stewart,
  Yet today if flew out of the bush, or out of his lines,
  To gather wool from my fair son's sweater.

THOUGHT

The instinct of this olive bird to gather fur
    From wallaby and man,
   Quite free from fear at nesting time,
   Is an instant of free thought as old as stone gods.

BAIAME

Baiame, the All-father, is a big fellow with a big dong
    And the rayed crown of a god.
   He looks at his Sunday children who snigger and drive
   Home to their home-units. The god is not surprised.

SRI RAMAKRISHNA ON MOUNT TOPHAM

By the cave of the hands a page blew on the wind
    To catch in thorn-flowers. Its message:
   Only those who see Divinity in all things
   May worship the Deity with advantage or safety.

A Betrothal

At Central Station seeing off Miss Watt,
('No Alfred, really I could not'
To green eyes and a red moustache)
Steam swept the asphalt. As the heads slid past,
A well-dressed man so far forgot
His senses as to board the train
In motion through a window helped by gloves,
By birds that hid a schoolgirl smile
While raising the dishevelled god,
To fly like Daphne through the groves,
Yet caught there before they turned to wood
Their modest owner said she might;

And waved above the daffodils
At Strathfield where suburban men
Astonished saw the god alight
To run beside the moving train
That blazed and whistled through the night.

Snake

The tiger snake moves
Like slow lightning. Like
A yard of creek water
It flows over rocks
Carving the grass.

Where have you gone,
Long fellow, cold brother,
Like a lopped limb or
Truth that we shy from
Leaving a cast skin?

Snakes are like a line
Of poetry: a chill
Wind in the noon,
A slalom in the spine
Setting ears back, hair on end.

'Some people will not live
With a snake in the house.'
Mice make off. Look
Under your chair; worse
Take down a book:

A line like an icicle!

Descent to Brindabella

For Jock Maxwell

The wagon moves like a snail,
The bullocks drawing out
Through the green timber.

The snail dips over a leaf;
And with wheels chocked
And sapling brakes between tree-trunks,
The canvas shell lurches down the east face.

The tree boles are ribboned
For eighty feet
Or scaled like goannas
That look up their full length
Through thin crowns below us.

Below us the valley waits
Like the first garden.
The river eats its way through green
Leaving a silvered snail-track,
And clouds snail over.
Their shadows slide through slippery blue
On the noon range.

And the wagon creaks and jolts:
Bullocks hang in their yokes
Bellowing, ball-eyed. One false
Move and the whole caboose
Could slip like water, pile up
Like debris in a treetop.

But the wagon inches with evening
Into the open valley dragging
Like a snail its humped shadow

Through the scents of mint and watercress
And the caress of water.

It has our house on its back.

Portrait of Mrs Deucher

'From Turalla to Manar
There was a koala in each tree;'
And her eyes were the colour
Of the skies of 1880

Seen through lean timber
(With a koala in each limb)
From the back of a leather buggy
That smelt of rain and housemaids.

'And Alexander at dinner
Told lies about lyrebirds
Dancing to lightning
As he rode through the Tinderrys.'

Tiny O'Keefe

Tiny O'Keefe said,
'I keep my coffin in my house.
It could hold all three of youse
Skinny buggers. Strike me dead!'

So they put down their glasses
And reeled uphill
To the red house he got
For burying dead 'uns.

The coffin filled the back porch. 'There's
A sweet piece of silky oak.
Pile in, you blokes.'
And he slipped home the latch.

Le Wombat

Voyage de Découvertes Aux Terres Australes
(Atlas par MM. Lesueur et Petit)

Le wombat inhabits the Ile King
Of Terre Napoléon
En Nouvelle Hollande.

L'île de l'artiste M. Lesueur
Is a scrubby cloud where
Le wombat bleu watches
La femelle rousse watching
While four enfants wombats terribles
Climb out of her pouch. Voilà!
Les wombats mère et père
Have the innocence of a magician
Producing un lapin blanc
From le chapeau noir.

If le père wombat bleu
Were to burrow in the shallow cloud
They would tumble tout de suite
Into le Golfe Joséphine. Les pauvres!

At l'ouverture de Golfe Joséphine
Is un pied-à-terre circumnavigated
By la corvette le *Géographe* in 1803,
Le capitaine, M. Baudin.

Ah l'Ile Decrés! where le casoar
Displayed his petites jambes bleues
And fine blue mutton-chops
Before his harlequin poulets. Hélas!
The dwarf emus of Kangaroo Island
Are only to be found today
Dans l'oeuvre de l'artiste M. Lesueur.

And la ville de Sydney
En Nouvelles Galles du Sud
With her moulins et boulangeries,
Her magasin de liqueurs fortes et de salaisons,
Mr Palmer's Woolloomooloo habitation,
Mr Campbell's débarcadère,
And the black Première Potence en Activité
Dans le Village de Brick-field,
The natives blowing coals
Among the stacked-up merchandise
By the Route de Parramatta?

Lunching above cloud
Above the murmur of the turning city
And the geographical outlines of
La ville de Sydney 1802 preserved
Dans l'atlas de l'artiste M. Lesueur,
We are moved by the innocence of the penal colony
As by le wombat français de l'Ile King
And les travaux executés dans le Golfe Bonaparte
A bord de la corvette le *Géographe*.
'Au fond de l'Inconnu pour trouver du *nouveau*!'

Two Views

For Lesueur aboard *Le Géographe* the scene
Was a kind of paradise. The swans are black
Pothooks butting haloes on a lake
Stippled and swept by wildfowl. On tender green
Banks, like picnickers beside the Seine,
In female poses kangaroos look back
At naked hunters fishing in a bark
Canoe the sacred waters in the sun.

Augustus Earle, in hell, thirty years on,
Depicts *A Native Family of New South Wales
Sitting down on an English Settler's Farm*.
The fallen king has rum to keep him warm
And Brisbane's jacket. On the verandah rails
The farmer straddles, pointing. Is that a gun?

Death in London

(Yem-mer-ra-wan-nie, d. 1794)

For Bennelong an opera house. The verger and beadle
Directed us to Yem-mer-ra-wan-nie's stone
By the 'public convenience' in Spencer Gardens Lane,
St John the Baptist, Eltham. What a redbrick hell
For a poor trapped heathen Aboriginal
Boy to leave his name and sacred bones in! –
Bennelong wrote, back home: 'Another black man
Took my wife away...He speared me...I am very well.'

121

There was a baptism at St John the Baptist
Of a Chinese Christian, and the Rev. Ned
Kelly officiated! On the first
Train back to town were four gold African girls.
'This white woman handed me a pound,' one said,
'From guilt!' And they laughed. – For Yem-mer-ra-wan-nie, bells!

from *Two Songs with Spanish Burdens*

I

A Grey Singlet

I was washing my lover's grey shearing singlet
When a squatter drew rein beside our quince tree
On a red impatient horse, with me at the copper:
And 'How much do you want for that stinking shirt?' says he.

Though his singlet is grey, his skin is a lily.

'A semi-trailer load of trade wethers would not buy it,
Nor a pen of prime lambs sappy from their mothers,
Nor a yarding of vealers with a leg in each corner,
Nor a mob of springing heifers with the dew on their nostrils.'

Though his singlet is grey, his skin is a lily.

'Not for a white homestead with a verandah all around it
And in vine-shade a waterbag of cool well water,
Thyme crushed on stone paths and bruised plums in the orchard,
Would I sell my lover's singlet to a show-off on horseback.'

Though his singlet is grey, his skin is a lily.

122

The Little Grebe

When moved in age to share a varied life
With his unworldly son
My father backed a horse between the shafts
Of an old gig – 'Whoa back!' – and off we spun.

He reined beside the rushes of a dam
But his eyes travelled on
Beyond the misted city to the range.
Late snow lay on Franklin.

And while he yarned, I watched the little grebe
Appear and disappear.
The dam filled up with clouds, and when the bird
Bobbed there again, the sky and dam were clear.

So I half-listened to my father's life,
Considering the grebe
And how it fed its feathers to its young
On rafts among the reeds.

Those floating incubators hatched the eggs.
Father, I did not know
Your shapely tales would wake in me in age
And fill my mind with distances and sorrow.

Words with a Black Orpington

The dark-haired girl said in the next
Life she would choose to be a chook:
'Like little black women
Fluffing themselves up...'
Bustling to see the – Excuse me! –
Lank gamecocks fight it out;
And scratching for innuendoes, nude
Earthworms of news.
Peck! – Sorry, my mistake.

A film slid over her bright
Brown convex eye. And click!
Went the Brownie Box. See her take the air
With six powder-puff yellow chicks
Under the clouded pears
And the hawk's hovering meditation.
– Watch for the dicky-bird, dears.

Like a fool, I said she'd likely
Wind up in a laying battery
With one thought a day, ovoid and smooth,
One tender thought to chuck about,
But when she turned
Like a thought it would be gone
Nodding around the production curve.

She lifted her elbows at that
And said she would be a homestead hen
With a nest under a damson plum
In the windfall orchard back home.
And I saw her calling, Chook, chook, chook!
And run helter-skelter towards herself.

And she buried her beak, once, in my neck.

Cigar Smoke

Skene tractoring day and night in tie and tweed hat
Smoking a cigar, a man silent like his land:
White sheep-tracks through belts of timber, water under sand,
Lean uplands moulded by creeks; and out beyond that
In storm-blue hills where lyrebirds danced, the hut
Of a bush hatter the nineties left behind.
'Evening, Mr Skene.' And the odd pair would stand
And gaze as one into blue distance. 'Got
That dingo's measure, but the bitch is sly.'
'You've all you need?' The smell of a cigar
Lingered in paddocks, and stockmen riding home
Snuffed early frost and winked: 'The boss rode this way.
You can smell him like a fox.' Warm firelight from
The homestead; defining space, the first chill star.

Blue Wren

The wren is a winged mouse.
Its cheeses fly
In a house full of holes.

The hips of the briar
Make a galaxy
Of dying orange stars.

The one living thing,
The wren on its violin
Frets out a song;

And the sun, that great oaf,
Like Jehovah cries from a cloud:
My son, my son!

125

Duchesses

A mob of dressing-tables is grazing
The pile of the plain
Under paper blue mountains.

Now and then one will pause
And raise its mirror
Reflecting the white sunlight.

Little cupboards
Hop in and out of the drawers
And suck at the crockery knobs.

The only sounds are the snip, snip,
Of grazing furniture
And the rattle of wooden droppings.

A truck is hurrying over the plain.
The mob raises its mirrors,
Little cupboards hop back in the drawers.

The dressing-tables head for the paper hills,
But the truck is upon them.
Pom pom! Corks fly from swivel guns.

Pomeranians snap
At the heels of the wheeling dressing-tables.
They snarl in mirrors, savaging the doilies.

The furniture is surrounded.
Men rope the younger pieces
And load them squealing onto the truck.

Now solitary in bedrooms
Dressing-tables look back at women
Who question them with rouge lips.

Sometimes through windows
They glimpse the paper blue mountains,
And the tears of the women fall on the doilies.

Wittagoona

Cave Paintings

He wore a mustard suit
And a sombrero
A tall sun-tinctured man
Full of an old man's stories
Of fashioning spears of supplejack
And whittling pipes from beefwood
In the shadowy caves
Stick figures in intricate designs
White red and yellow
Perform on the walls
Forgotten rituals
Warriors linked in a bird-dance
Hunters of delicate game
Emu transfixed phalanger kangaroo
A ladder pattern of dancing men
In corroboree
Perhaps an initiation
Though all is now conjecture
And all the while the tedious old man
Was whistling through a missing tooth
His lies of spearing duck on the wing
Among the red rocks and wonga vines
And leopard-woods of Wittagoona.

The Secret Life of a Leader

I was born in a wire house
They wrapped me in the wind's blanket
My mother's breasts were cans

On my birthday they gave me a rifle
My first love was a dead man's thought
Colours drained to black and white

My first duty was to my parents
They were shuffled away
                For my second lesson
I shot a close friend and the music master
They looked younger in death

My third task was at peak hour
                    Percussion
Hammered the subway
                    The gutters
Ran with red ketchup

They said I was ready
My vision spread like a virus
A crippled man blessed me

The city was gay with white flags
                    Skeletons
Cheered from the sidewalks
A schoolgirl presented a sheaf
Of spring flowers and fainted

When they unveiled the statue
I lost all movement in my right side

At my guarded chateau
Resting
          the trees kept rustling
They lopped the branches

I fished in a red river
And caught a beer can
At a farmhouse I rested

The farmer's wife curtsied
                    It was my mother
I picked up a hen egg
                    It blew my hand off
In the yellow nursery
                    I said I'd begin again

Mother tucked me in
And blew out the candle
Shh! she said
              What dreams you have!

James McAuley

Early in the Second World War, a young Sydney physician named Alfred Conlon persuaded the General Staff of the Australian Army to establish a hush-hush unit named the Directorate of Research and Civil Affairs, in order to save the nation's best minds from the front line and to undertake all manner of confidential tasks. Alumni of this unit would be influential in many spheres of Australian life for decades after the war, but differing political loyalties prevented them from being in any way a unified conspiracy. One of the young officers in this unit was a brilliant former scholarship boy named James McAuley, born the son of a builder in 1917. He had been trained by the outstanding philosopher John Anderson and had emerged with a top-flight MA, a rigorous mind, the scornful Sydney University debating style and a reputation both as a poet and as a tearing headlong player of the Dixieland piano. Contrary to the teachings of his mentor, McAuley would become a convert to the Catholicism his father had abandoned, and go on to be one of the leading Australian Catholic intellectuals of the pre-conciliar period. With the musician and lyricist Richard Connolly, he also would become the greatest Australian Catholic hymnodist of this century. The texts of two of his hymns are included in this selection.

While serving in the Directorate, James McAuley went to New Guinea to help restore and re-vamp Australian colonial rule in that country. Experience gained in this task led on to a post-war career as senior lecturer in the Australian School of Pacific Affairs. Also during his service in the Army, McAuley and another young lieutenant from his unit, Harold Stewart, spent an afternoon in mid-1943 concocting the persona and collected verse of a fictitious modernist poet named Ern Malley, a hoax intended to discredit the line being promoted by the Adelaide magazine *Angry Penguins*. This imposture was brilliantly successful, even though muddied at one point by farcical prosecution of passages in Ern's work which the police did not understand but thought might be obscene. Although he never existed, Malley survives fitfully as a quasi-political Elvis figure in Australian letters, and he did make the life of *Angry Penguins* editor Max Harris into something of a tragic anticlimax. After the war, McAuley published a closely argued anti-modernist book titled *The End of Modernity*, and he was consistently opposed to what he called the Magian heresy, which he saw embodied in all theories and movements that proposed to save mankind by human efforts. In 1956, he became founding editor of the anti-totalitarian magazine *Quadrant*, which still flourishes.

In 1961, James McAuley accepted a readership in poetry at the University of Tasmania, and subsequently became Professor of English there. In the 1950s and early 1960s, he strove at times rather grimly to reinstate a classical style, severely pruning all emotion except perhaps angry combativeness and, at times, writing as if the English eighteenth century were the wave of the future. Since this is a personal selection of his work, I have felt free to represent this professorial period in his work only sparingly. Like most readers, I prefer the rich diction of his early work and the breakthrough to gentler emotions that seems to have come after his poem 'Because'. James McAuley died in 1976 after a long and valiant fight with cancer.

Envoi

There the blue-green gums are a fringe of remote disorder
And the brown sheep poke at my dreams along the hillsides;
And there in the soil, in the season, in the shifting airs,
Comes the faint sterility that disheartens and derides.

Where once was a sea is now a salty sunken desert,
A futile heart within a fair periphery;
The people are hard-eyed, kindly, with nothing inside them,
The men are independent but you could not call them free.

And I am fitted to that land as the soul is to the body,
I know its contractions, waste, and sprawling indolence;
They are in me and its triumphs are my own,
Hard-won in the thin and bitter years without pretence.

Beauty is order and good chance in the artesian heart
And does not wholly fail, though we impede;
Though the reluctant and uneasy land resent
The gush of waters, the lean plough, the fretful seed.

Plumb

Nietzsche respected the great god Plumb
That lays his pipes in a baby's tum.
Beneath our logic's pure avowals
He heard the murmur of the bowels.

What beauty is, and truth, we learn
By gazing on that Grecian urn
The sovereign digestive tract,
Sole arbiter of faith and fact.

The colon is our River Nile,
Conduit of culture, the grand style,
And every barefoot god or nymph
Is nascent in our human lymph.

Plumb has the cosmos in his fist,
Thought's eternal pragmatist,
And poetry does what it can
To justify his ways to man.

Nietzsche respected the great god Plumb
Whose logos issues from his bum.

Landscape of Lust

Lust has its own country still
In which all lovers long to lie,
A land where each green-breasted hill
Touches the blue ecstatic sky
And the writhing limbs of trees
Are like our smiling energies.

The streams by natural alchemy
Transmute to laughter the rude shock
And thunder of the enormous sea;
And close as limpets to the rock
Our clinging bodies at their ease
Explore love's charming idiocies.

Delighted pleasure sinks to rest,
Then rises smiling, debonair,
To kiss each pouted lip and breast.
Then Vega charms the tumbling air;
For seated at bright Lyra's strings
She sings unmentionable things.

In country cabins, richly poor,
Where golden-headed wattle stands
Like an Apollo at the door
We make our lodging, and with hands
Inured to honest lovers' toil
We cultivate our living soil.

Terra Australis

Voyage within you, on the fabled ocean,
And you will find that Southern Continent,
Quiros' vision – his hidalgo heart
And mythical Australia, where reside
All things in their imagined counterpart.

It is your land of similes: the wattle
Scatters its pollen on the doubting heart;
The flowers are wide-awake; the air gives ease.
There you come home; the magpies call you Jack
And whistle like larrikins at you from the trees.

There too the angophora preaches on the hillsides
With the gestures of Moses; and the white cockatoo,
Perched on his limbs, screams with demoniac pain;
And who shall say on what errand the insolent emu
Walks between morning and night on the edge of the plain?

But northward in valleys of the fiery Goat
Where the sun like a centaur vertically shoots
His raging arrows with unerring aim,
Stand the ecstatic solitary pyres
Of unknown lovers, featureless with flame.

Ballade of Lost Phrases

In what museum now abide
The pamphlets that we read of yore;
Where are the orators that cried
'We will not fight a bosses' war,'
'The system's not worth fighting for,'
'To Hell with the Jingo profiteer,'
'The Empire's rotten to the core,'
– Where are the phrases of yesteryear?

No longer can it be denied,
The Left Book Club's become a bore;
We're social patriots double-dyed,
And social fascists too, what's more.
We tolerate Sir Samuel Hoare!
Churchill now delights the ear,
And Beaverbrook is to the fore.
– Where are the phrases of yesteryear?

The Party Line from side to side
Zig-zagged till our eyes were sore;
Can it be the Marxists – lied?
Peace to the shades of *Inprecorr*!
The left wing's moulting on our shore:
It will not fly again, I fear.
Freedom has become a whore.
– Where are the phrases of yesteryear?

Envoi

Comrades, we argued, fought and swore:
We might as well have stuck to beer.
The Japanese are in Johore
– Where are the phrases of yesteryear?

Revenant

I enter the familiar house
In which I worked and ate and slept
But twenty silent months ago.
Then at my voice the rafters leapt;
But now I stand and shout, hallo,

And there's no echo. Nothing moves.
The dust upon the floor lies still.
Grey coals are in the unswept grate.
The sunlight slants across the sill
On empty chairs. And here's a plate

With a bread-crust turned to mould; a glass
Stained with the dregs of wine. That's all.
One need not even be afraid.
There's nothing. Not even echo. Call
Again and see. But undismayed

I go out suddenly, as before,
Into the backyard overgrown
With twenty sullen months of weed;
Through the side-gate and down the road
For ever, no glance backward thrown,
Walking like a man that has been freed.

Jesus

Touching Ezekiel his workman's hand
Kindled the thick and thorny characters;
And seraphim that seemed a thousand eyes,
Flying leopards, wheels and basilisks,
Creatures of power and of judgment, soared
From his finger-point, emblazoning the skies.

Then turning from the book he rose and walked
Among the stones and beasts and flowers of earth;
They turned their muted faces to their Lord,
Their real faces, seen by God alone;
And people moved before him undisguised;
He thrust his speech among them like a sword.

And when a dove came to his hand he knew
That hell was opening behind its wings.
He thanked the messenger and let it go;
Spoke to the dust, the fishes and the twelve
As if they understood him equally,
And told them nothing that they wished to know.

Jindyworobaksheesh

By the waters of Babylon
I heard a Public Works official say:
'A culture that is truly Babylonian
Has been ordered for delivery today.'

By the waters of Babylon
A quiet noise of subsidies in motion.
'To a bald or mangy surface we apply
Our sovereign art-provoking lotion.'

By the waters of Babylon I heard
That art was for the people; but they meant
That art should sweeten to the people's mouth
The droppings from the perch of government.

The True Discovery of Australia

Erret, et extremos alter scrutetur Iberos

Let them wander and scrutinize the outlandish Australians
— THOREAU

Willem Jansz may well have been the first
To leave a bootprint on our shore, but he
Disqualified himself by being Dutch
From celebration in our history.

Dampier, that cool observant pirate,
Could fill an epic, and deserve the fuss;
But he, it seems, preferred the Hodmadods
And said that they were gentlemen to us.

138

Others, too, line up for epic treatment,
Discoverers of river-mouths and harbours;
But they must take their turn, as mortals do,
Who wait in beauty-salons or the barber's.

The one who now receives attention is,
Beyond all doubt, our True Discoverer,
Though verse has hitherto ignored his claim:
The glorious and forgotten Gulliver,

Who found his Lilliput where you will find
Lilliput still, and more so than before:
Close to Lake Torrens by his reckoning,
Though it has since expanded more and more

Till now the population-maps display
An acne rash, disfiguring the whole rind
Of white Australia, as she hugely squats
Above her pint-pot, fly-blown and resigned.

And whereas Gulliver has been neglected,
Hushed up almost, as of bad repute,
I here propose that we should change the name
Of Yorke Peninsula to Gulliver's Boot.

(For the benefit of readers overseas,
Not the steeple rising to a height
On pious Queensland, but the curious leg
That paddles in the south just near the Bight).

Since it is usual in histories
To make a contribution to research
By adding some new evidence or other,
I felt that Swift had left me in the lurch

By writing everything that could be known
About the great sea-captain; but I went

To Ida Leeson at the Mitchell, saying:
'I don't suppose you have a document. . . .'

Of course she had one! Had it there for years.
Near 'Phar Lap (see Houyhnhnms)' on the shelf:
A letter written to Lord Peterborough
And signed by honest Lemuel himself

In 1729; wherein he gives
The noble lord some further reasons why
He deprecates a recent move to float
A Lilliput Investment Company.

'The place, my lord, is much like Gideon's fleece
The second time he laid it on the ground;
For by the will of God it has remained
Bone-dry itself, with water all around.

'Yet, as a wheel that's driven in the ruts,
It has a wet rim where the people clot
Like mud; and though they praise the inner spaces,
When asked to go themselves, they'd rather not.

'The men are brave, contentious, ignorant;
The women very much as one expects.
For their religion, I must be excused,
Having no stomach to observe their sects.

'You must be wary in your conversation;
For, seeing them thumb-high, you might suppose
They recognised their stature, but beware!
Their notion of themselves is grandiose.

'And you will often find, although their heads
Are like a berry on a twig of bones,
They speak as Giants of the South Pacific
And treat the islands as their stepping-stones.

'North-east across the water, Brobdingnag
Casts its momentous shadow on the sea
And fills the sky with thunder; but they smile
And sit on their verandahs taking tea,

'Watching through the pleasant afternoons
Flood fire and cyclone in successive motion
Complete the work the pioneers began
Of shifting all the soil into the ocean.

'Sometimes they have to light the lamps at noon,
And seal their houses that are shipping dust
Like vessels in a storm; and truth to say
It is a kind of shipwreck. But they trust

'In providence: the Almighty's, not their own.
Meanwhile, as you'd expect, their arts are poor
As if the dust had leaked into their brains
And made a kind of dry-rot at the core.

'Knowledge is regarded with suspicion.
Culture to them is a policeman's beat;
Who, having learnt to bully honest whores,
Is let out on the Muses for a treat.

'Their Addison, their Swift, 's a magistrate.
Matters of aesthetics, courts determine.
Detectives play Petronius Arbiter
And hunt the poetasters down like vermin.

'The citizenry takes no part. For it,
Plato's a horse, Socrates a dog.
Surrounded by its vast domain, it sleeps:
A pigmy in the iron bed of Og.

'In prehistoric times the land was flat;
But then the mobile flange along the east

Buckled against the stubborn central shield,
Whereby a lowly mountain-range was creased.

'Mentally, they're still in Pliocene,
A flat terrain impermeably dense;
And will be so, until volcanic mind
Arches its back at brute indifference.

'The Southern Sea, my lord, in time to come
Will be the Bargain Basement of the earth,
With nations like demented women snatching
Remnants without enquiring what they're worth.

'Britannia may find herself obliged
To put a lot of oddments on the docket.
But you yourself, my lord, I should advise
To keep your money in your breeches' pocket.

'Your most obedient, L. Gulliver.'
Also, as Appendix B, I add
A recent find: a manuscript containing
Rejected verses of the Dunciad.

(Can this hard-mouthed, four-legged stanza trot
At such a stylish pace? I dare say not.
Yet here I make my verse a heliotrope,
Obsequiously proud, and follow Pope.)

'Let Fame's posterior trumpet sound once more!
Booksellers, make obeisance; bards, adore!
The King of Crambo, daubed with paint and smut,
A giant Nothing, comes to Lilliput.

'Th'egregious penguin, amorously blind,
Confuses oft a man with penguin-kind;
And at his feet, for reasons of its own,
Deposits, with quaint gravity, a stone.

'Less wonder, then, if now the silly bird,
By its own likeness gulled, adores th' absurd.
The huge Decoy inspires a solemn fuss
And to the tribe becomes eponymous.

'For lucid Ern, ye penguins, weep no more:
Henceforth he is the genius of the shore.
If, unawares, you stumble into sense,
His arm shall save, and your own impudence.

'Where'er th' Antarctic surge. . . .' But here a mouse
Has put his tooth to the historic scribble.
Would there had been a Vegetative Eye,
Or piece of Bread and Cheese, for him to nibble!

And the the mouse, my modest epic ends.
Gulliver refurbished takes the air.
Calliope, indifferent, says 'Who's next?'
And waves a customer into the chair.

But while the girl's not looking, I shall add
A private Envoi or reflective Coda
To readers fit though few: in a country where
An acorn-cup would seem a scotch-and-soda,

A man of even middling parts will look
So tall, he may forget his real status,
And play the sorry fable of the frog
Who burst his belly with his own afflatus.

Memorial

To Some Residents of New Guinea

When the sleeping isles were shaken
And many there bewildered fled,
Forsaking when they felt forsaken,
These no less bewildered made
Like reckoning of their chance, and stayed.
Hunted often and misled
By rumour, fear and stratagem,
Some died in horror without aid
And the years grow over them.
I write it brief and unadorned
That some remembrance may be paid
Far longer than they can be mourned.

To the Holy Spirit

Leaving your fragrant rest on the summit of morning calm,
Descend, Bird of Paradise, from the high mountain;
And, plumed with glowing iris along each curving wire,
Visit in time our regions of eucalypt and palm.

Dance, prophetic bird, in rippling spectrums of fire,
Ray forth your incandescent ritual like a fountain;
Let your drab earthly mate that watches in morning calm
Unseen, be filled with the nuptial splendours of your desire.

Engender upon our souls your sacred rhythm: inspire
The trembling breath of the flute, the exultant cosmic palm,
The dance that breaks into flower beneath the storm-voiced
    mountain;
Array in your dazzling intricate plumage the swaying choir.

144

Nativity

The thin distraction of a spider's web
Collects the clear cold drops of night.
Seeds falling on the water spread
A rippling target for the light.

The rumour in the ear now murmurs less,
The snail draws in its tender horn,
The heart becomes a bare attentiveness,
And in that bareness light is born.

New Guinea

In memory of Archbishop Alain de Boismenu, M.S.C.

Bird-shaped island, with secretive bird-voices,
Land of apocalypse, where the earth dances,
The mountains speak, the doors of the spirit open,
And men are shaken by obscure trances.

The forest-odours, insects, clouds and fountains
Are like the figures of my inmost dream,
Vibrant with untellable recognition;
A wordless revelation is their theme.

The stranger is engulfed in those high valleys,
Where mists of morning linger like the breath
Of Wisdom moving on our specular darkness.
Regions of prayer, of solitude, and of death!

Life holds its shape in the modes of dance and music,
The hands of craftsmen trace its patternings;
But stains of blood, and evil spirits, lurk
Like cockroaches in the interstices of things.

We in that land begin our rule in courage,
The seal of peace gives warrant to intrusion;
But then our grin of emptiness breaks the skin,
Formless dishonour spreads its proud confusion

Whence that deep longing for an exorcizer,
For Christ descending as a thaumaturge
Into his saints, as formerly in the desert,
Warring with demons on the outer verge.

Only by this can life become authentic,
Configured henceforth in eternal mode:
Splendour, simplicity, joy – such as were seen
In one who now rests by his mountain road.

Late Winter

The pallid cuckoo
Sent up in frail
Microtones
His tiny scale

On the cold air.
What joy I found
Mounting that tiny
Stair of sound.

To Any Poet

Take salt upon your tongue.
And do not feed the heart
With sorrow, darkness or lies:
These are the death of art.

Living is thirst for joy;
That is what art rehearses.
Let sober drunkenness give
Its splendour to your verses.

Move like the sable swan
On the luminous expanse:
In sight but out of range
Of barking ignorance.

By Your Kingly Power, O Risen Lord

(Refrain)

By your kingly power, O risen Lord,
all that Adam lost is now restored:
in your resurrection be adored.

1
Sing the joyful Easter cry,
sound it to the souls in prison,
shout our triumph to the sky;
sing Christ risen,
sing Christ risen.

2

Sing the joyful Easter cry,
let all times and peoples listen:
death has no more victory,
sing Christ risen,
sing Christ risen.

In Faith and Hope and Love

(Refrain)

In faith and hope and love
with joyful trust we move
towards our Father's home above.

1

Christ our star, our map, our road
to the Father's high abode.

2

Christ our bread along the way;
Christ our rescue when we stray.

3

Christ our shelter, Christ our friend,
our beginning and our end.

4

Christ our hope and our reward;
our redeemer and our Lord.

Warning

Beware of the past;
Within it lie
Dark haunted pools
That lure the eye
To drown in grief and madness.
Things that are gone,
Or never were,
The Adversary
Weaves to snare,
The mystery of sadness.

Fear to recall
Those terrible dreams
That sickened the heart
Or tore with screams
The shocked affrighted air;
Nor let your mind
Turn back to feel
The cold remorse
Nothing can heal,
Whose wisdom is despair.

Abandon the past;
Whoever gropes
For comfort there
Will lose his hopes.
The cruel memories stand
Like stone-faced gods
Watchful and grim,
Row upon row –
But raise them no hymn,
No sacrificing hand.

In a Late Hour

Though all men should desert you
My faith shall not grow less,
But keep that single virtue
Of simple thankfulness.

Pursuit had closed around me,
Terrors had pressed me low;
You sought me, and you found me,
And I will not let you go.

The hearts of men grow colder,
The final things draw near,
Forms vanish, kingdoms moulder,
The Antirealm is here;

Whose order is derangement:
Close-driven, yet alone,
Men reach the last estrangement –
The sense of nature gone.

Though the stars run distracted,
And from wounds deep rancours flow,
While the mystery is enacted
I will not let you go.

Companions

from Three Sonnets by Albrecht Haushofer

Today as into torpid dreams I sank,
I saw the whole crowd pass across the scene:
Saw Yorck and Moltke, Schulenberg, Schwerin,
Hassel and Popitz, Helferich and Planck –

Not one but of his duty was aware,
Not one but was to interest a stranger;
In glory and in power, in deathly danger,
They took the people's life into their care.

Look at them well: they are worth contemplating:
They all had intellect and rank and name;
On the same errand to these cells they came,

And for them all the hangman's noose was waiting.
At times rule passes to a madman's gang,
And then the best heads are the ones they hang.

Time Out of Mind

Time out of mind,
And out of the heart, too:
Yet I am not resigned
To be what I do.

Living, I seem to live
Outside my nature.
Giving myself, I cannot give
True form or feature.

In youth my range
Was fear, vanity, lust.
Shall I take in exchange
Fatigue, rage, self-distrust?

Only those joys that lie
Closest to despair
Are mine to hold on by
And keep me clear.

Yet at best or at worst,
This unknown self will see
What its Creator first
Thought it to be:

But I shall know this
Only in knowing
My self's Self, who is, and is
The end of my going.

Pietà

A year ago you came
Early into the light.
You lived a day and night,
Then died; no-one to blame.

Once only, with one hand,
Your mother in farewell
Touched you. I cannot tell,
I cannot understand

A thing so dark and deep,
So physical a loss:
One touch, and that was all

She had of you to keep.
Clean wounds, but terrible,
Are those made with the Cross.

One Thing at Least

One thing at least I understood
Practically from the start,
That loving must be learnt by heart
If it's to be any good.

It isn't in the flash of thunder,
But in the silent power to give –
A habit into which we live
Ourselves, and grow to be a wonder.

Some like me are slow to learn:
What's plain can be mysterious still.
Feelings alter, fade, return,

But love stands constant in the will:
It's not alone the touching, seeing,
It's how to mean the other's being.

Father, Mother, Son

From the domed head the defeated eyes peer out,
Furtive with unsaid things of a lifetime, that now
Cannot be said by that stiff half-stricken mouth
Whose words come hoarse and slurred, though the mind is sound.

To have to be washed, and fed by hand, and turned
This way and that way by the cheerful nurses,
Who joke, and are sorry for him, and tired of him:
All that is not the worst paralysis.

For fifty years this one thread – he has held
One gold thread of the vesture: he has said
Hail, holy Queen, slightly wrong, each night in secret.
But his wife, and now a lifetime, stand between:

She guards him from his peace. Her love asks only
That in the end he must not seem to disown
Their terms of plighted troth. So he will make
For ever the same choice that he has made –

Unless that gold thread hold, invisibly.
I stand at the bed's foot, helpless like him;
Thinking of the legendary Seth who made
A journey back to Paradise, to gain

The oil of mercy for his dying father.
But here three people smile, and, locked apart,
Prove by relatedness that cannot touch
Our sad geometry of family love.

The Sixth Day

Pollen on the tacky stigma,
Sperm loose-shining in the tide,
The deep join of need and pride
By which life pierces the enigma –

In you I find defined anew,
Not truly kept except in you;
And my flesh, having been made two,
Is one in what we are and do.

Our world's name is bliss;
I the firmament, you the earth,
Like sun and rain I am poured forth.

Enormously strange it is,
Forever to be you and I,
Not to die, not ever to die.

Confession

To know and feel are hard.
At times you are so much present
It seems I could touch your hand
And stand in your regard.

Mere fancies, but true enough;
And easy enough to lose,
As I abuse the moments,
And you accept the rebuff.

Small things do the hurt –
The lie vanity tells,
Malice or lust that die
Unacted in their dirt.

Bored in my self-prison,
I doubt uneasily;
But the times I get out,
I know you have risen.

Credo

That each thing is a word
Requiring us to speak it:
From the ant to the quasar,
From clouds to ocean floor –

The meaning not ours, but found
In the mind deeply submissive
To the grammar of existence,
The syntax of the real;

So that alien is changed
To human, thing into thinking:
For the world's bare tokens
We pay golden coin,

Stamped with the king's image;
And poems are prophecy
Of a new heaven and earth,
A rumour of resurrection.

Liberal, or Innocent by Definition

This is the solid-looking quagmire
The bright-green ground that tempts the tread
And lets you down into despond.

Enough consistence to conform,
Enough form to yield to pressure,
Enough force to wink at a fraud.

Unbiassed between good and evil,
The slander's only what they're told,
The harm something they didn't mean –

They only breathe what's in the air,
They have certified-pure motives,
So pure as to be quite transparent.

They are immune. Are innocent.
They can never be convicted,
They have no record of convictions.

This poem really needs a chorus
Spoken in dialect by the damned
Who live like frogs and have learned quagtalk:

'On the one hand this, on the other hand that,
Having regard to, I heard for a fact,
What one would want to say about this is,
That's not my point, and where are we at.'

In the Twentieth Century

Christ, you walked on the sea,
But cannot walk in a poem,
Not in our century.

There's something deeply wrong
Either with us or with you.
Our bright loud world is strong

And better in some ways
Than the old haunting kingdoms:
I don't reject our days.

But in you I taste bread,
Freshness, the honey of being,
And rising from the dead:

Like yolk in a warm shell –
Simplicities of power,
And water from a well.

We live like diagrams
Moving on a screen.
Somewhere a door slams

Shut, and emptiness spreads.
Our loves are processes
Upon foam-rubber beds.

Our speech is chemical waste;
The words have a plastic feel,
An antibiotic taste.

And yet we dream of song
Like parables of joy.
There's something deeply wrong.

Like shades we must drink blood
To find the living voice
That flesh once understood.

Numbers and Makes

The house we lived in faced the western line.
I used to sit and write the number down
Of every locomotive as it passed:
From the humdrum all-stations-into-town,

To the great thunderers that shook the house.
And passengers would wave back from the train.
I would watch out for when the signals moved
To stop or slow or all clear, and then strain

To catch the oncoming noise around the bend.
Or sometimes for variety I'd perch
Where I could note the make of every car
That passed along the street. Pure research,

Disinterested – but why, and into what?
There was no question then, no answer now.
Why change the memory into metaphors
That solitary child would disavow?

One Tuesday in Summer

That sultry afternoon the world went strange.
Under a violet and leaden bruise
The air was filled with sinister yellow light;
Tress, houses, grass took on unnatural hues.

Thunder rolled near. The intensity grew and grew
Like doom itself with lightnings on its face.
And Mr Pitt, the grocer's order-man,
Who made his call on Tuesdays at our place,

Said to my mother, looking at the sky,
'You'd think the ending of the world had come.'
A leathern little man, with bicycle-clips
Around his ankles, doing our weekly sum,

He too looked strange in that uncanny light;
As in the Bible ordinary men
Turn out to be angelic messengers,
Pronouncing the Lord's judgments why and when.

I watched the scurry of the small black ants
That sensed the storm. What Mr Pitt had said
I didn't quite believe, or disbelieve;
But still the words had got into my head,

For nothing less seemed worthy of the scene.
The darkening imminence hung on and on,
Till suddenly, with lightning-stroke and rain,
Apocalypse exploded, and was gone.

By nightfall things had their familiar look.
But I had seen the world stand in dismay
Under the aspect of another meaning
That rain or time would hardly wash away.

Because

My father and my mother never quarrelled.
They were united in a kind of love
As daily as the *Sydney Morning Herald*,
Rather than like the eagle or the dove.

I never saw them casually touch,
Or show a moment's joy in one another.
Why should this matter to me now so much?
I think it bore more hardly on my mother,

Who had more generous feelings to express.
My father had dammed up his Irish blood
Against all drinking praying fecklessness,
And stiffened into stone and creaking wood.

His lips would make a switching sound, as though
Spontaneous impulse must be kept at bay.
That it was mainly weakness I see now,
But then my feelings curled back in dismay.

Small things can pit the memory like a cyst:
Having seen other fathers greet their sons,
I put my childish face up to be kissed
After an absence. The rebuff still stuns

My blood. The poor man's curt embarrassment
At such a delicate proffer of affection
Cut like a saw. But home the lesson went:
My tenderness thenceforth escaped detection.

My mother sang *Because*, and *Annie Laurie*,
White Wings, and other songs; her voice was sweet.
I never gave enough, and I am sorry;
But we were all closed in the same defeat.

People do what they can; they were good people,
They cared for us and loved us. Once they stood
Tall in my childhood as the school, the steeple.
How can I judge without ingratitude?

Judgment is simply trying to reject
A part of what we are because it hurts.
The living cannot call the dead collect:
They won't accept the charge, and it reverts.

It's my own judgment day that I draw near,
Descending in the past, without a clue,
Down to that central deadness: the despair
Older than any hope I ever knew.

Tabletalk

In tabletalk my father used to tell
Of the escaped nun kidnapped by a priest;
Or innocent girls in the confessional,
Closeted in the dark with some gross beast.

By contrast, Anglican restraint was good:
It kept religion in its proper place. –
What all this talk was for, I understood
Only long after; but it left a trace.

In an unguarded moment once, I drew
Deserved rebuke for letting on I had
A plan of reading the whole Bible through:
He thought this a quick way of going mad.

On relatives my parents were agreed:
Too much association doesn't do,
And doubly so with the bog-Irish breed –
They're likely to want something out of you.

On friendship too the doctrine was as cold:
They're only making use of you you'll find;
Prudence consists in learning to withhold
The natural impulse of the sharing mind.

What is the wisdom that a child needs most?
Ours was distrust, a coating behind the eye
We took in daily with the mutton roast,
The corned-beef salad, and the shepherd's pie.

Self-portrait, Newcastle 1942

First day, by the open window,
He sits at a table to write,
And watches the coal-dust settle
Black on the paper's white.

Years of breathing this grime
Show black in the lungs of the dead
When autopsies are done;
So at least it is said.

Sunset over the steelworks
Bleeds a long rubric of war;
He thinks he knows, but doesn't,
The black print of the score.

He, like that sullied paper,
Has acquired no meaning yet.
He goes for long walks at night,
Or drinks with people he's met.

In sleeping panic he shatters
The glass of a window-pane.
What will he do with his life?
Jump three storeys down in the rain?

Something – guilt, tension, or outrage –
Keeps coming in nightmare shape.
Screams often startle the house:
He leaps up blind to escape.

By day he teaches the dullest
Intermediate class;
He gets on well with them, knowing
He too has a test to pass.

With friends he talks anarchism,
The philosophical kind,
But *Briefe an einen jungen
Dichter* speaks close to his mind.

Catherine Hill Bay 1942

White clouds twirled above us
Like the clean head of a mop.
Cattle found green pasture
To the brink of the cliff-drop.

Small violets and daisies
Were scattered through the grass.
Below the height, the water
Was green transparent glass.

The miners' little houses
Lined the narrow street;
And people sat on doorsteps,
The road beneath their feet.

The place was inbred and backward,
With enough evils there
For a dozen funny stories:
For once we didn't care.

Not yet rotted by artists,
Or some poetic tout,
That day it just existed
In time turned inside out.

Vale

for Ulick King

Greengrocer and black prince in shrilling choir
Respond from the dark trees that line the road
To the long throbbing cadence of desire
    That ends the Sapphic Ode.

I can still feel the keys and see the score;
You take time out to roll a cigarette;
I hear your crutches creak across the floor.
    You've nothing to regret:

You brought no accusation against life;
It was no crippled self you chose to wear,
And that warm courage drew to you a wife
    Most nobly fit to share

The sensual strength of deep organic love,
The root and thorn and crimson of the rose.
The end was a decline. What does that prove?
    There's no melodic close.

Your mother took you as a stricken child
To a faith-healer, hoping in despair.
Later she couldn't quite be reconciled
    As you outgrew her care.

But your great laughing strength was first her own;
And in those years when we were closest friends
She gave me kindness as another son.
    Somehow it never ends:

Kindness and courage like a stream flow on
Into the living. Grief dies out, the pain
Fades too. The honours that our flesh has won
    Like flowering trees remain.

The pulsing clang of the cicada choir
Fulfils the night: I am back thirty years;
Your voice throbs in the cadence of desire
    To silence beyond tears.

In the Huon Valley

Propped boughs are heavy with apples,
Springtime quite forgotten.
Pears ripen yellow. The wasp
Knows where windfalls lie rotten.

Juices grow rich with sun.
These autumn days are still:
The glassy river reflects
Elm-gold up the hill,

And big white plumes of rushes.
Life is full of returns;
It isn't true that one never
Profits, never learns:

Something is gathered in,
Worth the lifting and stacking;
Apples roll through the graders,
The sheds are noisy with packing.

Spider on the Snow

Gold fire, blue glaze; thin tangle of cirrus thread;
No stir of air, no bird's flight overhead.
The fleece of snow sweats crystal in the sun;
And secretly a thousand rivulets run
Sinking through lichened rocks, gurgling beneath
The matted alpines of the springy heath,
Till the plateau fills full and begins to spill
Far down the sides. But up here I crouch still,
Watching in astonishment a small
Dark-bodied red-legged spider steadily crawl
Across the snow, with no concern at all.

Anonymous Message

Believe O believe a native
Of the country of despair:
You must never give up hope,
Even just as something to wear.

The dry well choked with corpses
After the razzia, the need for flight,
The underground tricklings of pain,
The black empty wind all night –

They can't hinder, they even help:
Quite suddenly time uncloses
The most ancient, most fragrant, the most
Medicinal of all the roses.

Convalescence

Coffee and jasmine on a tray.
The stair resounds with feet to school,
Then fills with silence like a pool.
The world outside is windy grey.

A girl was strangled at Thirroul;
The market steadied yesterday.
I try to read, I ought to pray,
But lie and think how wonderful

To lift the phone or write a letter.
As I get well I grow more sure
(*Erbarme dich, du heiliger Retter*)

There's no relief or natural cure.
I drown in silence and endure
The thought of never getting better.

Late Sunday Afternoon

Muddy pools along the road
Mirror with a failing light
Grey ragged clouds and a pure height
Which at a passing wheel explode.

In the wet park July feels strange.
Bronze foil and russet overlap
New shoots of green. Black starlings clap
Their yellow beaks, announcing change.

Candles gleam, a bell is rung,
The faithful move towards the bread.
I shudder with desire and dread,
Tasting death upon my tongue.

Childhood Morning – Homebush

The half-moon is a muted lamp
Motionless behind a veil.
As the eastern sky grows pale,
I hear the slow-train's puffing stamp

Gathering speed. A bulbul sings,
Raiding persimmon and fig.
The rooster in full glossy rig
Crows triumph at the state of things.

I make no comment; I don't know;
I don't know what there is to know.
I hear that every answer's No,
But can't believe it can be so.

Madonna

Your head bent in the gesture of caring,
You hold the gold child aureoled
Against the blue sky of your breast.

Grace falls in folds. The child leans out
To bless the world. A derelict
Counts grains of prayer into the silence.

Give us back the images. And shut
The foolish mouths. Outside, a forewind
Whirls bits of paper, dust, dead leaves.

The sky runs cracks of jagged glare.

Music Late at Night

Black gashes in white bark. The gate
Is clouded with spicy prunus flowers.
The moon sails cold through the small hours.
The helpless heart says, hold and wait.

Wait. The lighted empty street
Waits for the start of a new day,
When cars move, dogs and children play.
But now the rigid silence is complete.

Again that soundless music: a taut string,
Burdened unbearably with grief
That smiles acceptance of despair,

Throbs on the very threshold of spring
In the burst flower, the folded leaf:
Puzzling poor flesh to live and care.

Francis Webb

Adelaide was the birthplace of Francis Webb, in 1925, but his mother died when he was only two years old, and he was brought up by his paternal grandparents in the comfortable Sydney suburb of Chatswood and educated at the Christian Brothers school there. In World War II he joined the Royal Australian Air Force, and his period of training in Canada led him to settle briefly in that country after the war. He then moved to England, and in 1949 suffered his first bout of schizophrenia. He was a well-loved patient in a number of hospitals in that country before returning to Australia in the early 1960s. Most of his remaining years were spent in mental hospitals and he died in 1973 at the early age of forty-eight.

Francis Webb's early artistic work embraced painting as well as poetry, and a number of small pictures which he painted in England are preserved in Willoughby Library, in Sydney. As his illness worsened, however, the painting fell away. The bulk of his writing, too, belongs to the period from the 1940s to the early 1960s. His reputation was made substantially by two large sequences based on characters from Australian history, *A Drum for Ben Boyd* (1948) and *Leichhardt in Theatre* (1952). Both are too long for our epitomizing purpose here, or indeed for the space available to us in this book, and both have proved resistent to excerpting. With his other sequences I have preferred to excerpt, in order to point to their existence and qualities, while concentrating on his individual shorter poems. The writing even of these faltered to a stop during the latter, terrible years of his illness, but a period of remission shortly before his death produced his 'Lament for St Maria Goretti', which is included here.

Some have considered Webb's poetry turgid, but others, including such good judges as Sir Herbert Read, have praised it in the very highest terms. Although he had a deep fear of Communism, exacerbated to nightmare pitch by his illness, he has been perhaps especially admired by radically-minded people in Australia. In his poetry and his tragic biography alike, he is perhaps the true Ern Malley, the tortured modernist figure some of them were looking for, but this time real, and a real poet. He might well have been puzzled by such an idea, and certainly his anguished heroism in the face of adversity is free alike of fiction or calculation. Even under the most pitiless assaults of his illness, he never lost his unassuming nobility of character.

To a Poet

Wayfarer, glorious one,
Heart fiery as a sun, lips stammering prophecies –
That you should pity me is credible, conceivable;
But it is unbelievable that I should pity you.

Yet don't you think, great one, in all your splendid journeys,
Your combats, your tourneys with this gangrened world of ours,
That there are some vignettes you may have overlooked, have lost,
Since you do not melt your mind's frost with any red-hot pennies?

Can those stern eyes, where beauty enters throbbing,
Have missed the conductor bobbing like a monkey on the tram?
Have your alert brain's sentinels been out setting pickets
Against the child chewing tickets, change rolling on the floor;

And factory girls on the early trains, rough badinage and chaff;
The ceremonial photograph, like a bottle circulating;
And the hordes of relatives, virago-tongued and vicious
(Irony most delicious!) over a ghost's furniture?

Now yours is the grand power, great for good or evil:
The schoolboy (poor devil!) will be told off to study you.
On hills over the sky you have set your plinths of stone;
You have crushed yourself, alone, in unscented, unstarred valleys.

You have fixed, fired a cresset that will always be alive;
I toil, delve, drive at my ballad blocks of roughness –
That you should pity me is credible, conceivable;
Exquisitely unbelievable that I should pity you!

172

Idyll

At noon the sun puffed up, outsize.
We saw a township on the rise;
Jack croaked 'A pub', then filed his throat,
Spat out an encroaching horde of flies.

One-headed Cerberus near the door
Bit off the fag-end of a snore,
Allowed us a red eye's filmy grace
And veiled the awful sight once more.

Sad barman showed a yellow fang;
Sweat was dirt-cheap, the whole place rang
A six-foot told a ten-foot yarn;
One chap was under, and one sang.

I'd bottle up that song without
A licence, just to serve it out,
A ballad, long and cool for days
Of epics, dry canteens, and drought.

We shouldered through the cork-tipped fog,
Paid several zacks and downed the grog;
Then like the brown fox of copperplate
Made exit over the lazy dog.

Morgan's Country

This is Morgan's country: now steady, Bill.
(Stunted and grey, hunted and murderous.)
Squeeze for the first pressure. Shoot to kill.

Five: a star dozing in its cold cavern.
Six: first shuffle of boards in the cold house.
And the sun lagging on seven.

The grey wolf at his breakfast. He cannot think
Why he must make haste, unless because their eyes
Are poison at every well where he might drink.

Unless because their gabbling voices force
The doors of his grandeur – first terror, then only hate.
Now terror again. Dust swarms under the doors.

Ashes drift on the dead-sea shadow of his plate.
Why should he heed them? What to do but kill
When his angel howls, when the sounds reverberate

In the last grey pipe of his brain? At the window sill
A blowfly strums on two strings of air:
Ambush and slaughter tingle against the lull.

But the Cave, his mother, is close beside his chair,
Her sunless face scribbled with cobwebs, bones
Rattling in her throat when she speaks. And there

The stone Look-out, his towering father, leans
Like a splinter from the seamed palm of the plain.
Their counsel of thunder arms him. A threat of rain.

Seven: and a blaze fiercer than the sun.
The wind struggles in the arms of the starved tree,
The temple breaks on a threadbare mat of glass.

Eight: even under the sun's trajectory
This country looks grey, hunted and murderous.

The Gunner

When the gunner spoke in his sleep the hut was still,
Uneasily strapped to the reckless wheel of his will;
Silence, humble, directionless as fog,
Lifted, and minutes were rhythmical on the log;

While slipstream plucked at a wafer of glass and steel,
Engines sliced and scooped at the air's thin wall,
And those dim spars dislodged from the moon became
Red thongs of tracer whipping boards aflame.

Listening, you crouched in the turret, watchful and taut
– *Bogey two thousand, skipper, corkscrew to port* –
Marvellous, the voice: driving electric fires
Through the panel of sleep, the black plugs, trailing wires.

The world spoke through its dream, being deaf and blind,
Its words were those of the dream, yet you might find
Forgotten genius, control, alive in this deep
Instinctive resistance to the perils of sleep.

For My Grandfather

When the ropes droop and loosen, and the gust
Piecemeal upon a widening quietness fails,
Fail breath and spirit; against the bony mast
Work in like skin the frayed and slackened sails.
In the green lull where ribs and keel lie wrecked,
Wrapped in the sodden, enigmatic sand,
Things that ache sunward, seaward, with him locked,
Tug at the rigging of the dead ship-lover's hand.
Though no wind's whitening eloquence may fill
Drowned canvas with the steady bulge of breath,

Doubling for past, for future, are never still
The bones ambiguous with life and death.

Dusk over Bradley's Head: a feeble gull
Whose sinking body is the past at edge
Of form and nothing; here the beautiful
Letona gybes, off the spray-shaken ledge.
And to those years dusk comes but as a rift
In the flesh of sunlight, closed by memory;
Shells stir in the pull of water, lift
Fragile and holy faces to the sky.
My years and yours are scrawled upon this air
Rapped by the gravel of my living breath:
Rather than time upon my wrist I wear
The dial, the four quarters, of your death.

The Black Cockatoos

Black cockatoos are somewhere under the sun:
Down with the mattocks, let the wild couch-grass run.
Take the gully-road, slide on the sticks and stones
And wait for the artists of Heaven, the crested ones.

Skinny growths of winter rouse themselves up
For a marriage, a picture, a poem. The cloth and the cup
Are lying upon the blue board. Music again,
Unearthly as space itself: they are coming, then.

With a full heart, kneel and accept what is given,
Take into your eyes and hearts this bounty of Heaven:
One prideful crow sidestroking brilliantly there
In somewhat less than a hundred feet of air.

The Song of a New Australian

In the hamper of a fictive world this wordy darkness
Is fed by the sick squeal of a truck moving
Onto a stage where friendly word means a weakness,
Safety hangs upon harlequin Hate with his gags
That are hallowed and hideous mockery of loving.
An interval – even armistice? But you only heard
A crate's bruising or breaking on concrete, then the last word
Of the damp, rolling, remorseless kegs.
Darling Harbour, self-fashioned, queer dogmas postered to his
    wall,
Discovers foreign all my words of defence,
Cannot have me in his black book, Mateship; so I fall,
Like the other thousands of mile-torn goods, to the phrases
Of the account-book, dump and stowage at a glance.
No relief from a galvanised-iron sea, and impure
Mouths are the sky-colours. Bridge is a coil of wire
Slung on top of some upturned filthy cases.

End of the Picnic

When that humble-headed elder, the sea, gave his wide
Strenuous arm to a blasphemy, hauling the girth
And the sail and the black yard
Of unknown *Endeavour* towards this holy beach,
Heaven would be watching. And the two men. And the earth,
Immaculate, illuminant, out of reach.

It must break – on sacred water this swindle of a wave.
Thick canvas flogged the sticks. Hell lay hove-to.
Heaven did not move
Two men stood safe: even when the prying, peering
Longboat, the devil's totem, cast off and grew,
No god shifted an inch to take a bearing.

It was Heaven-and-earth's jolting out of them shook the men.
It was uninitiate scurf and bone that fled.
Cook's column holds here.
Our ferry is homesick, whistling again and again;
But still I see how the myth of a daylight bled
Standing in ribbons, over our heads, for an hour.

Bells of St Peter Mancroft

Gay golden volleys of banter
Bombard the clockwork grief;
A frisson of gold at the centre
Of prayer, bright core of life.

Who knew the old lofty tower,
The ancient holy eye,
To come open like a flower,
To roll and wink with joy?

Townspeople, who wear
Shrewd colours and know the move,
Now blunder and wander, I swear,
In a transport of love.

And the belfry, hale and blest:
Picture the jolly hand
Milking each swinging breast
Of its laughing golden sound.

A Death at Winson Green

There is a green spell stolen from Birmingham;
Your peering omnibus overlooks the fence,
Or the grey, bobbing lifelines of a tram.
Here, through the small hours, sings our innocence.
Joists, apathetic pillars plot this ward,
Tired timbers wheeze and settle into dust,
We labour, labour: for the treacherous lord
Of time, the dazed historic sunlight, must
Be wheel in a seizure towards one gaping bed,
Quake like foam on the lip, or lie still as the dead.

Visitors' Day: the graven perpetual smile,
String-bags agape, and pity's laundered glove.
The last of the heathens shuffles down the aisle,
Dark glass to a beauty which we hate and love.
Our empires rouse against this ancient fear,
Longsufferings, anecdotes, levelled at our doom;
Mine-tracks of old allegiance, prying here,
Perplex the sick man raving in his room.
Outside, a shunting engine hales from bed
The reminiscent feast-day, long since dead.

Noon reddens, trader birds deal cannily
With Winson Green, and the slouch-hatted sun
Gapes at windows netted in wire, and we
Like early kings with book and word cast down
Realities from our squared electric shore.
Two orderlies are whistling-in the spring;
Doors slam; and a man is dying at the core
Of triumph won. As a tattered, powerful wing
The screen bears out his face against the bed,
Silver, derelict, rapt, and almost dead.

Evening gropes out of colour; yet we work
To cleanse our shore from limpet histories;
Traffic and factory-whistle turn berserk;
Inviolate, faithful as a saint he lies.
Twilight itself breaks up, the venal ship,
Upon the silver integrity of his face.
No bread shall tempt that fine, tormented lip.
Let shadow switch to light – he holds his place.
Unmarked, unmoving, from the gaping bed
Towards birth he labours, honour, almost dead.

The wiry cricket moiling at his loom
Debates a themeless project with dour night,
The sick man raves beside me in his room;
I sleep as a child, rouse up as a child might.
I cannot pray; that fine lip prays for me
With every gasp at breath; his burden grows
Heavier as all earth lightens, and all sea.
Time crouches, watching, near his face of snows.
He is all life, thrown on the gaping bed,
Blind, silent, in a trance, and shortly, dead.

The Brain-washers

They got the priest up before the court in session,
The crowd with their teeth brushed and bared, where he declared
That the Eucharist was a money-making superstition;

That he had murdered, corrupted, and sometimes hired
A few spotless working women of the parish.
He was one of the first. The glee was inspired,

For fatherly voices had been telling the town with a flourish
How the Church sucked blood from a scratching indigent land
Like some wily old insect overdue to perish;

That dogma was tenement wheezing in the wind;
Pointing out that many of the Sisters were plump beside
These dear little pupils – look, lift him with one hand –

That, in short, sin was the lust for material bread.
Maze of forest and a newly-turned-out fold,
They nosed round the magical gate. And he looked well-fed

Only his great round eyeballs rolled and rolled
Through stony raptures of the court, sank and ascended.
Of course no one had frightened this ugly child.

Truth to tell, he had no fear then, for the world had ended
Without fire or bang: there was never a murmured word
Once he started talking their way. And to be candid,

He may very likely have fought his fight a little too hard.
It took them over a year for something so simple
When he wandered in, proud and humble, with his God.

For the Brother in the cell beside him six months was ample:
He was dragged out screaming nothing. This taller man
Had climbed mountains in his time, was fond of the bodily
         temple.

When loudspeakers repeating a handful of words began,
And murmur and whisper wriggled in between,
He knew the greed of crevasse and placed a ban

Up personal downward thought. Only the evergreen
Pasture and young slopes of the Sacrament
Mounted daily to a white summit, unseen and seen.

So for months he was infuriatingly content,
Blessing the fellow who brought his mouldy bread;
Till at last the personal threaded that white ascent

And not quite Gethsemane satisfied the Lord.
Loudspeaker, murmur were every inch of the devil.
Of course the true will is a limb of Good,

And words and words can suggest an entire evil:
But here the observers gained their first point – curious,
He began to see the bringer of bread as his rival:

He must eat, but never lift his hand to bless.
His tired eyes lost their calm and he started singing
(This after months and months) in a breaking voice.

Some plateau within his mind was slipping, changing.
Because his nature was peace and climb and fight,
The voluptuous voices of the enemy were avenging

Themselves on his sleep, thinnest of veils, at night.
He repeated their words, twisted, and then on waking
Watched tiptoe spider's feet of uncanny light.

Outside was the world of loudspeakers, a dawn was breaking
With murmurings of birds round the narrow cell of life.
The priest was now always shivering and shaking,

Nor could the All-knowing soothe his waking grief.
For the words of half-sleep seemed real; a whispering wind
Swayed him over chasms of scandal, a tipsy leaf.

Every ear save One lusted for those words. At the end
He began to splutter, as a getaway, old gossip,
Sins of boyhood, tumbles of Alpine mind,

How once he'd have liked to strangle his own Bishop.
Such things were toys for indoctinate visitors,
They trundled them round the streets, draped in a cassock.

It is the frightened and conscious resistance that tires,
Though no one might venture to call it right or wrong.
When he repeated the loudspeaker's words – after years,

Centuries of bloom and murmur – silence came along.
It must be from God. He spoke often, feeling this,
And the words were the price of silence, worth anything.

So to the court. When judges had noted down
The needed words amid shocked delighted voices,
He simply mumbled the same words on and on –

A charity to the excited hungry faces.
As to his (they say) repentant, truthful confession:
It is cruel, but must tempt poetic airs and graces.

For the words meant nothing save only silence. A vision
Of man, perhaps, in his bitter search for peace.
Be angry; but notice almost an elation

In those rolling and rolling, uncontradicted eyes.

Five Days Old

For Christopher John

Christmas is in the air.
You are given into my hands
Out of quietest, loneliest lands.
My trembling is all my prayer.
To blown straw was given
All the fullness of Heaven.

The tiny, not the immense,
Will teach our groping eyes.
So the absorbed skies
Bleed stars of innocence.
So cloud-voice in war and trouble
Is at last Christ in the stable.

Now wonderingly engrossed
In your fearless delicacies,
I am launched upon sacred seas,
Humbly and utterly lost
In the mystery of creation,
Bells, bells of ocean.

Too pure for my tongue to praise,
That sober, exquisite yawn
Or the gradual, generous dawn
At an eyelid, maker of days:
To shrive my thought for perfection
I must breathe old tempests of action

For the snowflake and face of love,
Windfall and word of truth,
Honour close to death.
O eternal truthfulness, Dove,
Tell me what I hold –
Myrrh? Frankincense? Gold?

If this is man, then the danger
And fear are as lights of the inn,
Faint and remote as sin
Out here by the manger.
In the sleeping, weeping weather
We shall all kneel down together.

Hospital Night

(Second Version)

The side-room has sweated years and patience, rolls its one eye
Skyward, nightward; hours beyond sleep I lie;
And the fists of some ardent Plimsoll have laboured this wall
Clear of its plaster beside my chosen head.
Someone murmurs a little, dithers in bed.
Against that frail call
Are imminent the siege-works of a huge nightfall.

Trees, drawn up, rustle forward in the steep time of gloaming;
Crude green labours, gathers itself to a darkness, dreaming
Of perished ice-world summers, birds few, unwieldy, tame.
Darkness is astir, pondering, touching
Kinship with the first Dark in a trunk's crouching.
Darkness lays claim
To that vague breath-labour of a century, my name.

Someone calls again in his sleep, and my thought is pain,
Pain, till chanticleer will carol truce again
To the faceless joustings of green and green by an old cell,
With time roundabout, and labouring shapes of sin;
To the knotted fists of lightning, or tilting rain;
To the wind's lapse and swell
– Old die-hards of whom the birds shiver to tell.

Sleep is a labour amid the dilatory elder light;
But now a star is uttered in the long night,
Pitched beyond altercations of tree and storm;
For these, isled upon time, are murmuring, murmuring ever
Of good or evil becoming a darkness; but never
Darkens that star,
Housed in a glory, yet always a wanderer.

It is pain, truth, it is you, my father, beloved friend,
Come to me in the guile and darkness of a day's end,
As a frail intense blue burning, near nor far.
Old hands were stripped from the keyboard of time, they favour
White notes nor black, but they glitter and glitter of a lover,
As out of war
I labour, breathing deeply, and tremble towards your star.

from *Electric*

Song of the Brain

A mountainous countryside: ebbing away from the sun
Through Pia Mater's exquisite husbandry
Toils home the vision,
Through purling monotone of arteries, and frost-white pain
It gains the spare brow, storms time like a tree,
Arms all akimbo – and may perish in season.

How flows this sunset up the grey ransacked height,
Surging under old Pons Varolii, hazing
The patriarchal river?
Cloudbank and Hippocampus swim in light;
Among centuries of orange, passing, blazing,
Duyfken dreams of an island to discover.

What throe of spring is this? – music today,
Rolando's Fissure grumbles in travail.
And music's labouring form
Bears enigmatic fruit of sacrifice and joy.
Flowers and sheaves may cling to Ammon's Horn awhile.
Ptolemy groans for starlight in the storm.

Century and season: the unmerciful heavy clapper
Tells and toils dusk to last by-ways of the brain.
Come below the cerebellum;
Be wary of bat wings, shield your lighted taper.
Instinct, observe: the eroded figurine;
Memory – is it the sea we hear, so solemn?

Or tiny helot thoughts must sow and reap,
Make sterile tillage; or warm vines of love
Invade and shine.
Mutiny, mutiny – the whitecapped hordes of sleep;
Cry, music, sing us the golden seed alive
As Norman's brave and elegiac line.

Epilogue

In the gold doorway of dawn
Lurks the one-eyed raven,
Agile, of guile, looking down
On the sacred illness.

We are of an ancient stone,
Naked, with sunroad carven;
But crawls a yellow stain
Over the sacred illness.

Pain yawns, looms;
Sin is bawdily woven,
We would shrug from our draped limbs
The sacred illness.

But the black doorway of our curse
Returns golden, forgiven
By the electric Cross
And the sacred illness.

Brave works of truth assail
The stone unfaced and cloven,
Man must clasp to his soul
The sacred illness.

from *Eyre All Alone*

8 *Aboriginals*

All my days and all my nights
You haunt me.
Once came a yell or shriek at eleven exactly.
Joy, or welcome? Cowering, I peeped at the rifle
That will not fire. Once in the hungry scrub
Leaves and branches came together as a shadow,
Made a sleekness rippling, running about out of earshot.
Innumerable times the great Expedition of my thought
Has gone to pieces,
Frightened horse galloping in all directions.

You are everywhere at once.

My instinct is to shudder away from you.
Love? It is for dry bread like a stone in my mouth,
For petty concentric days stemming from me,
For stars all white abroad in my fame,
For sleep crawling solicitously towards me,
For myself at all ages since I began walking.

These days I hardly say a word to Wylie.

You are beyond me – and so often
Dangerously close, it seems. I do not look for
Truce, rule of life; but gratefully follow your footprints
To water, water on the fifth day.

Walk, walk. From dubious footfall one
At Fowler's Bay the chosen must push on
Towards promised fondlings, dancings of the Sound.
Fourth plague, of flies, harries the bloodless ground.
Cliff and salt balance wheel of heathen planet
Tick, twinkle in concert to devise our minute.
But something on foot, and burning, nudges us
Through bitter waters, sands of Exodus.

10   *Banksia*

History, wasted and decadent pack horse
Munching a handful of chaff, dry old national motives,
Shambles skinny and bony into the final push,
Picking up, putting down his heavy tuneless hooves
Girt with rusted iron, so tenderly.

Baxter is dead. Wylie, can you hear the Sound?

I hear large agnostic ribaldries of an ocean.

Evening in muffler creeps towards epic adventure,
To lull the blazing colossi of a blindness.
But suns will rock in my sleep, maul the moth-eaten pockets
Of memory for a few counterfeit coppers
To thump on the counters of stalls in a looted market.

Wylie, what can you see?
                              I see a flower.

Turn the horses loose. Out of earth a power:
Banksia, honeysuckle, forked-lightning-fruit of pain.
Motive pierces the cloud-scrub once again.

Swimming oversea, underfoot, the brawny light
Sings savour of this unique approaching night.
Stolid elation of a single star.

Banksia, carry fire, like the thurifer
Over my sandy tongue-tied barren ground

Wylie, what do you hear?
                    I hear the Sound.

Senor Hirsch and the God

Nostromo crouched in the shadows:
One lighted window above him impressed again
Up his parcelled senses man the empirical:
Prophetic postmarks of man
Were stamped numbly upon his padded paper solitariness,
His near-humility. With man wakened paranoia, wars,
Stagehand refugees, busy, unpicturesque,
Streaming in all directions, in a huddle as proper delta;
And ultimate burned the buried ingots, the buried ingots,
The real, the god, the screenplay.

Genesis of these entertainments? Some remnant of Senor Hirsch
Grown quieter, colder. Yes, drunken with terror,
He had babbled entreaties to Baal – or to himself:
He knew in alto rhapsody of terror his dictator flesh
Lash its arms up so high above its own head.
Dangling almost cruciform he must deliberate a little;
And queerly enough, despair cannot bear silence's
Legitimate tradings with hides, comings and goings:
So despair whipped up to him. Senor Hirsch lifted his head,
Spat in the face of his torturer, spat in his own face,
And died renouncing his terror, renouncing himself.

The mystery being that he died not by his own hand,
And that his slung demented shadow threatens the ingots, the
    ingots.

Around Costessy

1   Hastings

Pasture, embryo hills,
The Dwelling by the Waterside,
Cotesia, open eye.
Improvident Harold has died:
The two neutral ravenous mills
Munch apathetic rye.
Buried the old laissez faire.
Totalitarian herald,
Domesday Book, and banner
Deride the schoolboy Harold,
Twirl militant arms in the air,
Munch ecstatic florin and tanner.
So four strict carucates of land;
Villein, villein, villein;
Pannage for one hundred hogs
(Illiterate Harold is slain);
Bordars, plough-teams to hand
With the secret documents, logs.
Give us fourteen sure head of cattle
Escheating to Crown, State, Power;
Welcome recoinnoitring groups.
History halts but one hour,
All the Harolds must die in battle
Before the indoctrinate troops.

2   Our Lady's Birthday

Eleven o'clock. Reservoirs of Heaven,
Waters of the sun,
No-colour; and a rippling
Before the prospecting nervous eye.
And a tenderness wherein Calvary is begun
And sunset foreboded, a tenderness coupling

191

White heat with goldenness; and the seven
Rainbow sorrows; and the urchin sea
Clambering about; and the haystack library,
Academic decorous morocco and vellum
Bound, stalled in the heavy light upon a calm.

For the Immaculate as for Original Sin
It is pain to begin:
From womb of grace to pedantic midwife earth,
Sharp oxygen-needles plotting in her two old hands;
Then a breast of valour made vagueness as the sky
Over automation's oceans and rifled lands.
So these the hours of your birth
Transcribe a primitive sacred agony;
But you are the child crying, small rapture and paroxysm
In the lewd snake-bodied wind.

And you are an arch hurled across the wicked chasm
By your Playfellow, of the matchless mind.

Song of Hunger

I lie extended on my canvas bed.
Blowzed sun squats on his hunkers overhead
To lick the mealy bowl of heaven dry.
Soon in the town's back streets, I must be dead,
But not while one cloud is loafing in my brain
As that fragrant unleavened Bread
Which may not die.

Carbohydrate, sugar, fat, protein
Are finite but as crucial as tropic rain;
So the sacked larder of manhood hazards mice

Of memory, infant voices: foetal grain
Puts on a blossom's child-cajoleries;
And the grey skinflint plain
Is lost in rice.

Mistake not, lives are in me, mysteries
Of throbbing corn and spectral orchard trees.
To empty bowels and airy compunctions give
Daylight, one thousand thousand calories.
I loom at nightfall, surfeited with grace.
Fall on your knees, your knees,
For, man, I live!

So carouse with charity, hurry to this place,
My splayed eternity for your embrace:
Hold up the anna's fiery Host, and call,
See life's spotless calligraphies crease my face
While rickety skeletal shanks work up above
Canvas, space-platitude, race
To His tiny stall.

O my love, O my love!

Airliner

I am become a shell of delicate alleys
Stored with the bruit of the motors, resolute thunders
And unflagging dances of the nerves.
Beneath me the sad giant frescoes of the clouds:
Towerings and defiles through intense grey valleys,
Huge faces of kings, queens, castles – travelling cinders,
And monuments, and shrouds.
A fortress crammed with engines of warfare swerves.

193

As we bank into it, and all the giant sad past
Clutches at me swimming through it: here
Is faith crumbling – here the engines of war
In sleek word and sad fresco of print,
Landscapes broken apart; and here at last
Is home all undulant, banners hanging drear
Or collapsing into chaos, burnt.
And now we are through, and now a barbarous shore.

Grimaces in welcome, showing all its teeth
And now the elder sea all wrinkled with love
Sways tipsily up to us, and now the swing
Of the bridge; houses, islands, and many blue bushlands come.
Confine me in Pinchgut, bury me beneath
The bones of the old lag, analyse me above
The city lest I drunkenly sing
Of wattles, wars, childhoods, being at last home.

Derelict Church

When earth and flint rear themselves into certain shapes
There is prayer from the fiery centre of the earth:
That grey dancer the belfry vaulting as the Host,
Arches as mouths importunate.
Dun smoking flames come leisurely home to roost,
The lost mind slews to an enigmatic path
Joining hands again, the errant spirit leaps
Into fire of joy at this grimy Fishergate.

Over the river's dank effluvia
Hang like launches the oozing sunsets, palls
Of light close dully. Enter this crippled church
To pray with a near pride:

Cases are piled in the transept and the porch
Yet peace loiters here as not in cathedrals
While with advertisement and trivia
Man is besieging Heaven for his trade.

The Cross slopes down to jackboot and grimy truck;
Bones of the dead are indifferent to our debris
Grating above them; the devouring sin and pain
Still come to burial;
The immemorial Shape is persistent as rain.
Ghosts of bells chatter as from the sea
Out of memory slides home this gaping wreck
Still seaworthy, hallowed, and functional.

Ward Two

1 *Pneumo-encephalograph*

Tight scrimmage of blankets in the dark;
Never fluxions, flints coupling for the spark;
Today's guilt and tomorrow's blent;
Passion and peace trussed together, impotent;
Dilute potage of light
Dripping through glass to the desk where you sit and write;
Hour stalking lame hour...
May my every bone and vessel confess the power
To loathe suffering in you
As in myself, that arcane simmering brew.

Only come to this cabin of art:
Crack hardy, take off clothes, and play your part.
Contraband enters your brain;
Puckered guerrilla faces patrol the vein;
The spore of oxygen passes

Skidding over old inclines and crevasses,
Hunting an ancient sore,
Foxhole of impulse in a minute cosmic war.
Concordat of nature and desire
Was revoked in you; but fire clashes with fire.

Let me ask, while you are still,
What in you marshalled this improbable will:
Instruments supple as the flute,
Vigilant eyes, mouths that are almost mute,
X-rays scintillant as a flower,
Tossed in a corner the plumes of falsehood, power?
Only your suffering.
Of pain's amalgam with gold let some man sing
While, pale and fluent and rare
As the Holy Spirit, travels the bubble of air.

2   *Harry*

It's the day for writing that letter, if one is able,
And so the striped institutional shirt is wedged
Between this holy holy chair and table.
He has purloined paper, he has begged and cadged
The bent institutional pen,
The ink. And our droll old men
Are darting constantly where he weaves his sacrament.

Sacrifice? Propitiation? All are blent
In the moron's painstaking fingers – so painstaking.
His vestments our giddy yarns of the firmament,
Women, gods, electric trains, and our remaking
Of all known worlds – but not yet
Has our giddy alphabet
Perplexed his priestcraft and spilled the cruet of innocence.

We have been plucked from the world of commonsense,
Fondling between our hands some shining loot,
Wife, mother, beach, fisticuffs, eloquence,
As the lank tree cherishes every distorted shoot.
What queer shards we could steal
Shaped him, realer than the Real:
But it is no goddess of ours guiding the fingers and the thumb.

She cries: *Ab aeterno ordinata sum.*
He writes to the woman, this lad who will never marry.
One vowel and the thousand laborious serifs will come
To this pudgy Christ, and the old shape of Mary.
Before seasonal pelts and the thin
Soft tactile underskin
Of air were stretched across earth, they have sported and are one.

Was it then at this altar-stone the mind was begun?
The image besieges our Troy. Consider the sick
Convulsions of movement, and the featureless baldy sun
Insensible – sparing that compulsive nervous tic.
Before life, the fantastic succession,
An imbecile makes his confession,
Is filled with the Word unwritten, has almost genuflected.

Because the wise world has forever and ever rejected
Him and because your children would scream at the sight
Of his mongol mouth stained with food, he has resurrected
The spontaneous thought retarded and infantile Light.
Transfigured with him we stand
Among walls of the no-man's-land
While he licks the soiled envelope with lover's caress

Directing it to the House of no known address.

Saboteur autumn has riddled the pampered folds
Of the sun; gum and willow whisper seditious things;
Servile leaves now kick and toss in revolution,
Wave bunting, die in operatic reds and golds;
And we, the drones, fated for the hundred stings,
Grope among chilly combs of self-contemplation
While the sun, on sufferance, from his palanquin
Offers creation one niggling lukewarm grin.

But today is Sports Day, not a shadow of doubt:
Scampering at the actual frosty feet
Of winter, under shavings of the pensioned blue,
We are the Spring. True, rain is about:
You mark old diggings along the arterial street
Of the temples, the stuttering eyeball, the residue
Of days spent nursing some drugged comatose pain,
Summer, autumn, winter the single sheet of rain.

And the sun is carted off, and a sudden shower:
Lines of lightning patrol the temples of the skies;
Drum, thunder, silence sing as one this day;
Our faces return to the one face of the flower
Sodden and harried by diehard disconsolate flies.
All seasons are crammed into pockets of the grey.
Joy, pain, desire, a moment ago set free,
Sag in pavilions of the grey finality.

Under rain, in atrophy, dare I watch this girl
Combing her hair before the grey broken mirror,
The golden sweetness trickling? Her eyes show
Awareness of my grey stare beyond the swirl
Of golden fronds: it is her due. And terror,
Rainlike, is all involved in the golden glow,
Playing diminuendo its dwarfish rôle
Between self-conscious fingers of the naked soul.

Down with the mind a moment, and let Eden
Be fullness without the prompted unnatural hunger,
Without the doomed shapely ersatz thought: see faith
As all such essential gestures, unforbidden,
Persisting through Fall and landslip; and see, stranger,
The overcoated concierge of death
As a toy for her gesture. See her hands like bees
Store golden combs among certified hollow trees.

Have the gates of death scrape open. Shall we meet
(Beyond the platoons of rainfall) a loftier hill
Hung with such delicate husbandries? Shall ascent
Be a travelling homeward, past the blue frosty feet
Of winter, past childhood, past the grey snake, the will?
Are gestures stars in sacred dishevelment,
The tiny, the pitiable, meaningless and rare
As a girl beleaguered by rain, and her yellow hair?

Nessun Dorma

In Memory of Jussi Bjorling

Past six o'clock. I have prayed. No one is sleeping.
I have wandered past the old maternity home's
Red stone fermented by centuries; and there comes
New light, new light; and the cries of the rooks sweeping
To their great nests are guerrilla light in a fusion
– Murmurs, echoes, plainsong; and the night
Will be all an abyss and depth of light between
Two shorelines in labour: birth and death. O passion
(One light in the hospital window) of quickening light,
O foetus quaking towards light, sound the gaunt green,
Trawl Norfolk, make shiver the window-blind,
Harass nebulae for Bjorling. Find him, find.

And now the bar, the feeble light, glissade
Of tables and glasses, and the mantel-set
Intoning his death. Broad tender sunlights fret
Our twilight, his remembered voice has laid
Cock-crow and noon upon harrowed palms of the sill.
O broad light and tender, lucent aria,
Lacerate my paling cheeklines with the steep
Bequest of light and tears, flood me until
The man is the dawning child; be anathema
To man-made darkness. No one, no one shall sleep
Till the cry of the infant emergent, lost and lame,
Is the cry of a death gone towering towards the Flame.

Lament for St Maria Goretti

Six o'clock. The virginal belly of a screen
Winces before the blade, the evening wind:
Diluted, a star
Twitches like a puddle on scoured hygienic stone.
All of the documents signed and countersigned
And truce to a cruel war:
Wreckage gesticulates, toothless broken ships,
Meteorite, cherubim. Horseman, in the wash of space
Round the petty bays of this child's face.

Teresa, it is easier now. But the choloroform
Comes like a stiletto to our gasping void:
Sometimes you look lovely swimming there beside me
I would take you into my hands to remould you, shape you,
But the pain, the pain . . .

                See Teresa, my father Luigi is coming
Out of the cemetery (but the chloroform holds) shouldering away
The earth. He touches his little Cross with his lips,
I am crying, and a flight of birds hangs like a rosary,
He is smiling, but the chloroform will dissolve him . . .

Six o'clock. The bells of Nettuno chime
Angelus: Ave to Ave, hand to hand
The buckets of sound are passed in a slow time
Up to a thirsting land.
Again the breeze at the hospital window flutters in lace
Near the thirsting wilderness of this child's face.

Touch me, Teresa: you know you often asked me
Why I was in tears at Mass before the Communion:
I seemed to see Him there, heaving up to Golgotha,
And rising and falling, I stood there mocking Him
Like when I stole two spoonfuls of Angelino's polenta
(You haven't committed a sin, said the kind old priest):
Three times He fell: the last note of the Angelus
Falls with Him – I am falling with Him
– Must I fall with Him into chloroform?
Take up your cross. Touch me, Teresa, quickly . . .

Six o'clock. There may be a moon tonight.
At dead Ferriere twitches the comatose star.
A peasant knows the early mosquito bite
Like a stiletto into his wincing ear.
The suave impersonal light
Trails its skirts over marshland: no mourners here,
And Nothing mourns at Nettuno: feel the embrace
Of Nothing scrambling ashore at this child's face.

Teresa, he's coming: *don't, you will go to Hell* . . .
Teresa, I can still see you: Ferriere is closing in:
The chloroform works at you. Be dainty Corinaldo
Where I was born. I can hardly read or write:
But your breast is our little pet hill, your hair like shadows
Of clouds on our grain, your mouth like a watercourse.
Have you spoken? have words of water been truly uttered
To my thirst – it's this drumming, drumming in my ears.
Teresa, I am going. Teresa, to the last be Corinaldo,
All life writing me on earth:

Let my hands reach you – I can hardly sign my name:
My signature, my scrawl: now wait, Teresa, Teresa...

Six o'clock. And the Miserere. Final Grace.
And Death and the Woman, strangely at one, will place
Ambiguous fingers on all of this child's face.

Bibliography

Kenneth Slessor *One Hundred Poems*, Sydney, Angus & Robertson, 1944 seq. Copyright © Paul Slessor.

Roland Robinson *Selected Poems*, ed. Robert Gray, Sydney, Angus and Robertson, 1989; *Alcheringa*, A.W. and A.H. Reed P/L; *Deep Well*, Sydney, Edwards and Shaw P/L; *Poet's Choice*, Island Press, 1976; *Selected Poems*, Armidale, Kardoorair Press, 1978. Copyright © the Estate of Roland Robinson.

David Campbell *Collected Poems*, ed. Leonie Kramer, Sydney, Angus and Robertson, 1989. Copyright © Mrs Judith Campbell.

James McAuley *Collected Poems*, Sydney, Angus and Robertson, 1980; *The New Living Parish Hymn Book*, ed. J.A. de Luca, Sydney, E.J. Dwyer P/L 1986 seq. Copyright © Mrs Norma McAuley.

Francis Webb *Cap and Bells: The Poetry of Francis Webb*, ed. M. Griffith and J. McGlade, Sydney, Angus and Robertson, 1991. Copyright © A.L. Meere, C.M. Snell, M.A. Webb-Wagg.

"Carcanet are doing an excellent job in this series: the editions are labours of love, not just commercial enterprises. I hope they are familiar to all readers and teachers of literature."
— *Times Literary Supplement*

Border Ballads: a selection
edited by James Reid

Poetry by English Women:
Elizabethan to Victorian
edited by R.E. Pritchard

The Poorhouse Fugitives:
Self-taught poets & poetry in
Victorian Britain
edited by Brian Maidment

AKENSIDE, MACPHERSON & YOUNG
Selected Poetry
edited by S.H. Clark

MATTHEW ARNOLD (1822-1888)
Selected Poems
edited by Keith Silver

WILLIAM BARNES (1801-1886)
Selected Poems
edited by Robert Nye

APHRA BEHN (1640-1689)
Selected Poems
edited by Malcolm Hicks

THOMAS BEWICK (1753-1828)
Selected Work
edited by Robyn Marsack

EDMUND BLUNDEN (1896-1974)
Selected Poems
edited by Robyn Marsack

THE BRONTË SISTERS
Selected Poems of Charlotte,
Emily and Anne Brontë
edited by Stevie Davies

ELIZABETH BARRETT BROWNING
(1806-1861)
Selected Poems
edited by Malcolm Hicks

THOMAS CAMPION (1752-1770)
Ayres and Observations
edited by Joan Hart

THOMAS CHATTERTON (1752-1770)
Selected Poems
edited by Grevel Lindop

JOHN CLARE (1793-1864)
The Midsummer Cushion
*edited by R.K.R. Thornton
& Anne Tibble*

Cottage Tales
*edited by Eric Robinson, David
Powell & P.M.S. Dawson*

ARTHUR HUGH CLOUGH (1819-1861)
Selected Poems
edited by Shirley Chew

SAMUEL TAYLOR COLERIDGE
(1772-1834)
Selected Poetry
*edited by William Empson
& David Pirie*

ANDREW MARVELL (1621-1678)
Selected Poems
edited by Bill Hutchings

JOHN MASEFIELD (1878-1967)
Selected Poems
edited by Donald Stanford

GEORGE MEREDITH (1828-1909)
Selected Poems
edited by Keith Hanley

WILLIAM MORRIS (1834-1896)
Selected Poems
edited by Peter Faulkner

JOHN WILMOT, EARL OF ROCHESTER
(1648-1680)
The Debt to Pleasure
edited by John Adlard

CHRISTINA ROSSETTI (1830-1894)
Selected Poems
edited by C.H. Sisson

DANTE GABRIEL ROSSETTI (1828-1892)
Selected Poems and Translations
edited by Clive Wilmer

SIR WALTER SCOTT (1771-1832)
Selected Poems
edited by James Reed

MARY SIDNEY, COUNTESS OF
PEMBROKE (1561-1621)
& SIR PHILIP SIDNEY
The Sidney Psalms
edited by R.E. Pritchard

SIR PHILIP SIDNEY (1554-1586)
Selected Writings
edited by Richard Dutton

JOHN SKELTON (1460-1529)
Selected Poems
edited by Gerald Hammond

CHRISTOPHER SMART (1722-1771)
The Religious Poetry
edited by Marcus Walsh

HENRY HOWARD, EARL OF SURREY
(1517-1547)
Selected Poems
edited by Dennis Keene

JONATHAN SWIFT (1667-1745)
Selected Poems
edited by C.H. Sisson

ALGERNON CHARLES SWINBURNE
(1837-1909)
Selected Poems
edited by L.M. Findlay

ARTHUR SYMONS (1865-1945)
Selected Writings
edited by R.V. Holdsworth

JEREMY TAYLOR (1613-1667)
Selected Writings
edited by C.H. Sisson

THOMAS TRAHERNE (1637?-1674)
Selected Writings
edited by Dick Davis

HENRY VAUGHAN (1622-1695)
Selected Poems
edited by Robert B. Shaw

OSCAR WILDE (1854-1900)
Selected Poems
edited by Malcolm Hicks